DIARY
OF A
BILINGUAL
SCHOOL

DIARY OF A
BILINGUAL
SCHOOL

*How a Constructivist Curriculum,
A Multicultural Perspective, and
A Commitment to Dual Immersion Education
Combined to Foster Fluent Bilingualism
In Spanish- and English-Speaking Children*

Sharon Adelman Reyes
&
James Crawford

 DiversityLearningK12
PORTLAND, OREGON

For permission to reprint, send email to:
info@diversitylearningk12.com

Or send postal mail to:
DiversityLearningK12
P. O. Box 19790
Portland, OR 97280

ISBN 978-0-9847317-0-1
Library of Congress Control Number: 2011941003

Library of Congress Subject Headings:
1. Education, bilingual—Study and teaching (Elementary).
2. Second language acquisition—Study and teaching (Elementary).
3. Constructivism (Education)—United States.
4. Immersion method (Language teaching).
5. Bilingualism in children.

Cover photograph by Sharon Adelman Reyes
Book design and typography by James Crawford
Printed in the United States of America
First edition
10 9 8 7 6 5 4 3 2 1

To the Founders of Inter-American

**Adela Coronado-Greeley
and Janet Nolan**

*without whose vision, energy, and dedication
this story would not have been possible*

In Memoriam

Benancio Villegas, Jr.
1988–2011

Contents

�֍ �֍ �֍

Preface

❦ ❦ ❦

By Sharon Adelman Reyes

THIS BOOK GREW OUT OF MY EXPERIENCE as a parent first, an educator second. Or, more precisely, it was born out of my frustration with bilingual schooling options for my children. I felt it was important for them, coming from a biracial, bilingual, and bicultural family, to feel at home in two worlds. And language seemed to be an obvious bridge between their Puerto Rican and Jewish identities. So I enrolled my older child, Andre, in a Chicago elementary school that offered Spanish-as-a-second-language classes. Sadly, the program failed to excite him. After six years of instruction, my son still showed limited interest or proficiency in the language.

I was determined that my daughter, Glenna's, experience would be different. She spent her preschool and kindergarten years in Spanish-predominant classrooms, where she thrived and I was delighted. After kindergarten, I asked that she remain with her classmates in the transitional bilingual program. While the school administration thought this a bit odd, given my daughter's English-language dominance, my request was ultimately granted.

Then, in the autumn of Glenna's first-grade year, I began a series of visits to her classroom, pursuing interests that were both personal and professional (by now, I was a PH.D. candidate in education). What I discovered no longer delighted me. I entered a classroom in which childhood was silenced by a rigid curriculum devoid of creativity and thoughtful instructional planning, an environment in which conformity was mandated and "discipline" maintained at all times.

The morning routine typically began with the children copying a teacher-created story from the chalkboard. Next came a phonics lesson, followed by children's recitations from a Spanish-language basal reader.* A few minutes were then devoted to answering literal comprehension questions regarding the text, usually involving the sequence of events. Finally, the children would be asked to take out their notebooks and draw a picture of the story.

On some days, as the thirty or so children sat silently drawing their pictures, the teacher called on them, one at a time, to sit and read to her at the back of the room. Soon the teacher's aide would begin to circulate among the other students, distributing ditto sheets for them to color and giving instructions on how to fill in the pictures. This would last for up to forty-five minutes, until it was time for a bathroom break.

With the exception of lunch and a short recess, the children remained at their desks all day for more phonics drills, science lessons taken from a text, and other seatwork. The only verbal communication between students that was allowed occurred in the lunchroom and on the playground. The store-bought and teacher-made displays that decorated the room all portrayed smiling white children, with no references to Latino cultures. And remember, this was a Spanish-English bilingual program!

The occasional music class consisted of a room with five straight rows of desks and chairs, without instruments or any space for physical activity. The children sang songs in English, in sequential order, from a cassette tape. Throughout one session the teacher spoke in cold, stern tones: "I really don't like all this noise. I want you to settle down and be quiet. I can't start with all this talking." She sent one child to the back of the room for speaking. He sat underneath the table where I was seated and remained there, forgotten, for the next half-hour.

Visiting Glenna's classroom was becoming an exercise in frustration. Prefabricated Halloween decorations were replaced by similar images of Thanksgiving. The daily regimen of teacher-directed activities continued.

---

*Basal readers consist of stories, poems, and other writings, usually abridged or revised, that are designed to teach specific literacy skills in a preplanned sequence. Unlike authentic children's literature, they generally fail to excite students about reading.

Nonetheless, I forced myself to return each week, although my visits became increasingly shorter. One November day the teacher led a discussion, a rare event in that classroom. The level of excitement rose as hands flew up and children vied for the opportunity to participate. Soon the discussion wound down, but the children did not. The teacher walked over to a girl and forcefully closed her book, slamming the pages shut. Then she faced a boy nearby who was still talking, placed her hand on his upper arm, and visibly tightened her grip until he, too, became silent. Order was restored.

I began to lie awake at night, thinking about what was going on—and not going on—in Glenna's classroom. When seeking a bilingual education for my daughter, I had considered only language; now I was forced to consider educational philosophy as well. I spoke to the principal, but he refused to acknowledge that there was anything problematic about the school's approach. I felt paralyzed, reluctant to give up on Glenna's chances to become bilingual, yet horrified by what she was experiencing.

One evening after school, Glenna informed me that if she finished her homework she could move ahead and do extra pages in her workbook. She was proud that she was further ahead in her workbook than any of the other students. She was good. She listened to the teacher. She was not like the bad kids who talked.

"You don't have to be good all of the time. Sometimes it's okay not to be so good," I told her. My daughter looked at me quizzically. I had the urge to tell her to talk in class, to get some answers wrong on her paper, to speak her mind. But I recalled how the teacher ensured obedience and I bit my tongue.

Clearly, it was time to look for a new school. I decided that, if I had to choose between second-language learning and a meaningful education for Glenna, I would choose an all-English school with an appropriate early-childhood curriculum.

Fortunately, I never had to make that choice. By the end of November, I was able to arrange for Glenna's transfer to Inter-American, a public dual immersion school. My visit to her future classroom had featured an energetic and friendly teacher surrounded by active children exploring a classroom environment full of books, manipulatives, and art materials.

Soon I learned that these features were typical of the school, the result of a long history of language, instructional, and curricular planning.

Inter-American was born out of the vision of two teacher-parents who wanted a progressive bilingual education for their own children and for the children of others, and who were willing to engage in a grassroots effort to achieve that goal. Here Glenna began her re-education, learning that school need not be about being "good," listening to the teacher, and giving the correct answer. It could be about discovering new worlds, posing her own questions, and exploring independent interests. Meanwhile, I began to reconsider the role of curriculum in second-language classrooms.

What's more, I could not forget the callous treatment of Glenna's former classmates, predominantly working-class children of immigrant parents. My daughter had escaped, but they had not, and that basic injustice continues to trouble me.

This book is about children of diverse ethnic, racial, cultural, and socioeconomic backgrounds who were fortunate enough to land in a school where both language and curriculum matter; where children are free to grow both bilingually and intellectually. It is about the ways in which language learning and curriculum combine in dual immersion classrooms to promote schooling that children enjoy, that inspires confidence in parents, and that allows educators to co-create and learn alongside their students. It is about rethinking pedagogy in dual immersion education. Above all, it is written in the hope that more children—whether bilingual, multilingual, or monolingual—will someday benefit from a *constructivist* education.

DIARY
OF A
BILINGUAL
SCHOOL

❦ INTRODUCTION ❦

A Year in the Life

We need a sense of hope in our assessment of schools and our work in them. Not blithe optimism, but a grounded belief that something can be done: some image of goodness and some tangible sense of how to begin.

—Mike Rose*

SOME READERS MAY BE EAGER TO KNOW how dual immersion education can be "aligned" with the latest standards, tailored to federally mandated testing programs, or held accountable for meeting "benchmarks" of student achievement. If so, they should put down this book and look elsewhere. The public discourse on schooling today is far too concerned with such distractions. In our view, these fashionable notions of "education reform" have nothing to do with real teaching and learning, bilingual or otherwise. We believe they are passing fads that will eventually run their course. One can only hope that will occur before America's schools are severely damaged.

This book, by contrast, is about *possibility*. Depicting a year in the life of a second-grade classroom, it demonstrates what can happen when the instruction is bilingual and the curriculum is constructivist. Children thrive in an environment that unlocks their intellectual curiosity and enthusiasm for learning. Simultaneously, without conscious effort,

*Source notes begin on page 115.

they become proficient in two languages and at home in a culture that differs from their own.

Their story unfolds at the Inter-American Magnet School in Chicago, Illinois. The program was one of the country's earliest and most acclaimed experiments in dual immersion, thanks to the strong commitment of parents as well as educators and an adventurous approach to pedagogy. Much has been written about the virtues of this model—and this particular school—in nurturing bilingualism and biculturalism for students from diverse backgrounds. Yet surprisingly little attention has been paid to its progressive educational philosophy, curriculum, and methodology. Exploring how these priorities complement and strengthen each other is the central focus of this book.

We present it here in the form of day-to-day narratives, each followed by a brief discussion of what transpired and how the children responded. Our aims are twofold: first, to convey the immediate experience of a bilingual constructivist classroom and, second, to analyze that experience and its impact on student learning.[*]

We begin with an overview of dual immersion and constructivism, along with a brief synopsis of their guiding principles. Five narrative chapters follow, illustrating how the principles were applied by a talented teacher. A final section tracks the lives of the main characters into the present, to see how the former second-graders are faring today as young adults.

While the theoretical portions of the book are grounded in research, references will be kept to a minimum in the interest of accessibility for readers, whether laypersons or professionals. Source notes at the end of the volume will provide suggestions for further reading.

Some Notes on Terminology

BILINGUAL EDUCATION IS KNOWN for its abundance of terms, often contradictory and confusing to nonspecialists. Here, for the sake of clarity, is a brief glossary of those that appear in this book.

---

[*]The classroom and family narratives are taken from an ethnographic study conducted during the 1995–96 school year. These stories were collected through audio recordings (transcribed by native speakers of the languages used), still photography, and detailed field notes.

We use *dual immersion* to refer to a pedagogical model sometimes described as "dual language," "two-way bilingual education," or "two-way bilingual immersion." Such programs enroll children of at least two different linguistic backgrounds and are bilingual in both goals and methodology.

Immersion—as distinguished from *submersion,* or "sink or swim"—encompasses various strategies for teaching a second language through "sheltered" instruction in academic subjects. The term is also commonly used to describe "one-way" program models serving students from a single language background, such as Spanish immersion for English speakers.

English language learners (ELLs)—also known as "emergent bilinguals" or, formerly, as "limited-English-proficient" students—are children from minority language communities in the United States who are still in the process of acquiring proficiency in the majority language.

Developmental bilingual education, sometimes described as "bilingual maintenance," is a program designed to teach English to ELLs while also supporting the development of their native language. As with dual immersion, the goals are proficient bilingualism and grade-level (or better) academic performance.

Transitional bilingual education, by contrast, is an approach designed to promote English acquisition for ELLS as quickly as possible, while using students' native language only to the extent necessary until they can be reassigned to mainstream, all-English classrooms.

English as a second language (ESL) and *Spanish as a second language (SSL)* describe various programs designed to foster second-language acquisition in a context where the *target language* is a widely spoken vernacular in the surrounding community rather than a "foreign" tongue.

PART I

Fundamentals

SOMETIMES IT SEEMS that every educational method, strategy, or fad these days is being touted as "research-based." Variations on that magical phrase appear more than a hundred times in the No Child Left Behind Act of 2001, directing schools to use "scientific" evidence to guide their efforts and expenditures. As a result, quantitative data are now invoked to justify all manner of instructional approaches, but especially those designed to boost scores on standardized tests.

The reality is that, in the field of education, definitive studies of pedagogical effectiveness are rare. There are so many variables that must be controlled in evaluating real-world programs that "generalizable" findings can be elusive. A model that works in one context, for one group of students, under one style of teaching or leadership, may fail in others. And vice versa. In addition, there are value judgments about the aims of schooling that can never be supplied through "data-driven" decision-making.

By contrast, basic research on child development and language acquisition, along with practical experience and a willingness to experiment, offer a starting point for designing programs that teach the whole child. These are the factors that combined at the Inter-American Magnet School to produce an innovative blend of dual immersion and constructivism.

❦ CHAPTER ONE ❦

Making Sense of the Words — and the World

Knowing a second language ... enhances creativity and academic success, it makes connections between generations stronger, and it allows an individual to connect with more of the world. It is a "boundary eraser" in all senses of the word.

—Kendall King and Alison Mackey

FLUENT BILINGUALISM IS COMMONPLACE throughout much of the world. How strange that it's so difficult to achieve in the U.S.A.! Unless we came here as immigrants, grew up in homes where another language was spoken, or spent extended time in a non-English-speaking country, most Americans are likely to be monolingual. Not a devastating handicap—English is dominant internationally and becoming more so—but hardly an optimal condition, either. Despite the controversy it sometimes arouses, bilingualism has indisputable advantages: social, cultural, academic, professional, even cognitive. The evidence is clear: Speaking two or more languages not only enriches our lives; it can also make us smarter and more successful. Recognizing these realities, increasing numbers of Americans are seeking effective language-learning opportunities for themselves and especially for their children.

Our public schools are finally beginning to respond. Over the past twenty years, language immersion programs have mushroomed, both "one-way," involving students from a single language background, and "two-way," involving speakers of both target languages. While immersion models vary considerably in details, they have generally proven far more successful than the foreign-language classrooms that most of today's parents were forced to endure. Rather than teaching skills out of context—remember the flash-cards, grammar exercises, artificial dialogues, and other mind-numbing activities?—well-designed immersion programs help students acquire a second language by using it for meaningful purposes, including subject-matter instruction. Such classrooms turn out graduates who tend to be much better at actual communication in the target language—more likely, for example, to converse easily with native speakers in real-life situations. These advances were made possible, in large part, by pedagogical insights gained from bilingual education programs for language-minority students in the United States and for language-majority students in Canada.

There's another factor that also deserves mention: advocacy by determined parents, working in concert with educators who were able to contribute professional expertise and a willingness to take risks. Without such alliances, it's unlikely that experiments in dual immersion would have ever been tried.

Origins of Dual Immersion

THE FOUNDERS OF CHICAGO'S INTER-AMERICAN Magnet School, Janet Nolan and Adela Coronado-Greeley, were both parents and educators. As parents, they organized community members to put pressure on the Chicago Public Schools and the Illinois State Board of Education. As professionals, they were able to access the growing research base on bilingualism to help with program design.

Janet had spent time teaching English as a second language (ESL) in Mexico, where she was impressed by young children's capacity for language learning. She was also inspired by the work of Theodore Andersson, a pioneering researcher in the field of bilingual education, who stressed the benefits of early literacy in two languages. Fluent in Spanish, though a nonnative speaker herself, Janet created a bilingual environment at home for her two preschool-age daughters. The initial results were promising. Yet it soon became clear that, to continue nurturing their Spanish development, more institutional support would be needed to balance the predominance of English outside the home.

Adela, a Mexican-American from East Los Angeles, was a community organizer who also worked at a school on Chicago's South Side. Though she had grown up speaking Spanish, she recognized that her own children faced similar obstacles as Janet's in becoming truly bilingual. So the two parent-educators joined forces to create what would become Inter-American.

Over a several-year period, they led campaigns to secure grant funding, find a building, hire teachers and aides, purchase books and materials, arrange transportation, and ultimately create a permanent dual immersion program. Their advocacy paid off when the Chicago Public Schools approved a bilingual preschool in the fall of 1975. Because of funding constraints, however, it was open to Latino students only. The next year a kindergarten classroom was added, the following year a first grade. Official designation as a magnet school, serving children from all language groups, finally came in 1978. The name *Inter-American*, suggested by the parent of a Spanish-dominant student, was quickly adopted.

Meanwhile, Adela and Janet drew on the pedagogical breakthroughs achieved in French immersion programs introduced in Quebec in the mid-1960s. Anglophone students there started school, learned to read, and were taught academic subjects in French, with lessons carefully adjusted to their level of proficiency. A class in English language arts was introduced in second grade, but most instruction continued in French. By the end of sixth grade, students achieved functional competence in the second language, at no cost to their academic progress when measured in English—a remarkable accomplishment. It turned out that, under the right conditions, bilingualism could be acquired incidentally and naturally. Over the years, variations of French immersion have become so popular that they now enroll approximately 317,000 Anglophone students throughout Canada.

Yet the one-way immersion model also has its limitations. Because English-speaking students rarely interact with native speakers of French, they often have difficulty developing native-like proficiency in French or close relationships with Francophone peers. At Inter-American, by contrast, the founders brought together children from Spanish- and English-language backgrounds, creating an educational environment that was both bilingual and bicultural.* By learning together in the same classrooms, students from each group acquired a second language more effectively and also forged cross-cultural friendships and understanding. From the school's beginnings, it embraced diversity, socioeconomic as well as racial and ethnic, while stressing respect for the two languages and the two language communities. Not surprisingly, Inter-American also encouraged the active involvement of parents, who were welcomed as an integral part of the school community and who participated in most important decisions affecting children. By the 1990s, it enrolled more than six hundred students from prekindergarten through eighth grade.

Initially, instruction was provided half in English and half in Spanish, a policy that required all teachers to be fully bilingual. This "50-50" model is common in dual immersion programs, often in response to parents' anxieties. If my child is taught mostly in another language, they wonder, how will she keep up academically in English? While the concern is understandable, research shows it is largely unfounded. In well taught bilingual and immersion programs, whether one-way or two-way, the skills and knowledge that students acquire in one language easily "transfer" to another. Reading ability, for example, is something that children need to learn only once; it can then be applied to each new language they acquire.†

By 1990, it became clear that Inter-American students were doing quite well in English, but their Spanish proficiency was lagging. The founders recognized that the minority language, which had limited support outside of school, especially for English-dominant students, needed a stronger emphasis in the classroom. So they adopted an "80-20" ratio

*In practice, children from more than two linguistic and cultural backgrounds often participate in dual immersion programs. The most common ethnic group represented at Inter-American in the 1990s—after Latino, African-American, and non-Hispanic white—was Vietnamese.

†The transfer effect is well documented even between writing systems that differ widely, such as Chinese and English or Turkish and Dutch.

of Spanish to English from prekindergarten through fourth grade, combined with ESL and SSL (Spanish as a second language) as needed.* Until
the end of second grade, children were taught reading primarily in their
native language. This was the dual immersion model during the 1995–
96 school year in which our story takes place, and it proved quite successful. Academic outcomes at Inter-American have been impressive,
with students from both language groups scoring well above city and
state norms in English and Spanish.

Beyond Language

WHAT HAS FURTHER DISTINGUISHED dual immersion schools like Inter-
American, contributing to their successes, is a break with traditional,
teacher-centered classrooms in favor of constructivist approaches that
guide rather than prescribe what children learn. In many ways, this
change has been less a conscious choice than a practical necessity.

Transmission models of education, which are designed to "deliver"
a predetermined body of knowledge and skills, treating children as passive receptors of "content," simply don't work well when it comes to
learning languages. Witness the failure of traditional foreign-language
classes to cultivate functional bilingualism. The same could also be said
of most "transitional" bilingual classrooms, which seek to push children
into English as quickly as possible, at the cost of neglecting their native-
language development. It is no coincidence that this "subtractive" bilingual approach tends to favor transmission models as well, using "drill
and kill" methodologies in the false hope that they will speed up English
acquisition.

Dual immersion programs have often proved superior, both in pro-
moting fluency in two languages and in fostering academic learning.
This has been true in large part because they require children to become active learners. Instead of drilling students in formal aspects of
the target languages (phonics, grammar, vocabulary, spelling, punctua-
tion), dual immersion relies on using the two languages for meaningful
purposes. As children focus on subjects that excite them—the world of
insects, for example—and on interacting with peers from a different

*In grades 5–8, the ratio shifted to 50-50.

culture, bilingualism comes naturally. In this way, the classroom environment creates a strong motivation to learn. Equally important, it gives students the key that unlocks proficiency in a second language: meaningful communication in that language, also known as *comprehensible input.*

The term was coined by Stephen Krashen, an influential researcher whose work has helped to shape programs for English language learners over the past generation. While the linguistics—rooted in the theories of Noam Chomsky—may seem complex, the basic idea is simple. We acquire a second (or third) language in much the same way as we acquire our first. Not by studying grammar books or memorizing vocabulary lists or "practicing" verbal skills, but by *receiving and understanding messages* in a new language.

To ensure that children are receiving comprehensible input, dual immersion teachers use various techniques—physical cues, pictorial aids, or simplified vocabulary, for example—to make instruction as accessible as possible. Students acquire both language and subject matter as they "construct meaning" from what they experience. Hence the term *constructivism.* This principle applies not only in language education but, more broadly, in an approach to curriculum that builds on instead of undermining students' innate desire to make sense of the world—that is, to learn.

> *[Humans] acquire language in one fundamental way. We acquire language when we understand it. What is spectacular about this idea is that it happens incidentally, involuntarily, subconsciously, and effortlessly.*
>
> —Stephen Krashen

Constructing Knowledge

RATHER THAN AN EDUCATIONAL STRATEGY or a methodology, constructivism can best be described as a philosophy of knowledge and how it is acquired. In other words, it is a theory about how "knowing" takes place. Drawing on the work of developmental psychologists Jean Piaget and Lev Vygotsky, constructivists conceive learning as a process of reconciling prior knowledge and understandings of the world with new experiences and social interactions, resulting in new knowledge and new understandings.

This insight has profound implications for education. If knowing is inherently subjective—the product of activity occurring in the minds of individual learners—then it cannot be transmitted directly from teacher to students by means of lectures, worksheets, homework, quizzes, and similar devices. Of course, facts and formulas can be loaded into children's short-term memory, where some of these items may be retained until the next round of multiple-choice tests. But true learning only occurs when students are stimulated to think critically, to build and rebuild their own mental models of reality, to achieve a deeper understanding. Or, as early-childhood educator Beverly Falk puts it, "Learning is something that a learner does, not something that is done to the learner."

Thus constructivism values questioning, reasoning, analysis, reflection, problem-solving, cooperation, and creativity among the intellectual assets that children will need in school and in life beyond school. As such, it stands in sharp contrast to *behaviorism,* a philosophy that defines learning as an externally directed activity: the acquisition of desired behaviors through repetition and reinforcement. Explicitly or otherwise, behaviorist assumptions guide most transmission models of education. In particular:

- that a predetermined body of knowledge and skills can be broken down into component parts, then taught in logical sequence;
- that student progress toward mastery of the curriculum can be measured at various points on a linear continuum from "below basic" to "advanced";
- that behavioral competence—ability to recall knowledge or employ routine skills—is the primary goal of schooling; and
- that external rewards (grades, prizes, recognition) are essential in motivating students to learn.

Entirely missing from the behaviorist framework is the concept of *cognitive change.* Nor is there any place for self-directed learning, the intellectual growth that occurs through experiences and discoveries that challenge prior perceptions of the world. Instead, behaviorists promote preconceived notions of "what students should know and be able to do"—

deceptively described as "standards"—around which curriculum must be designed and "achievement" must be measured.

Scaffolding and Sheltering

CONSTRUCTIVISTS, BY CONTRAST, believe that the fundamental challenge for educators is to create an open and stimulating environment that is conducive to learning. Toward that end, classroom instruction must take into account what Vygotsky calls the "zone of proximal development," the gap between what a child can already do and what he or she can potentially accomplish when given appropriate assistance from teachers and collaborating peers. That assistance can take the form of *scaffolding* or *sheltering.*

Scaffolding enables students to reach higher levels of problem-solving than they could achieve independently—in effect, providing a series of manageable steps on which to climb. It might include introducing key concepts, asking questions to encourage observation or analysis, modeling the structure of a narrative, organizing collaborative teams, or performing a practical demonstration. For the constructivist educator, the function of scaffolding is not to steer students toward the "correct" answer, but to provide them with temporary supports until they are able to pose questions and discover answers on their own. The goal is not to avoid making errors. Indeed, discussing and analyzing children's misconceptions in the classroom can be a powerful form of scaffolding, to the extent that it enables them to discard their original concepts in favor of new, more viable ones.

Sheltering may be defined as a form of scaffolding adapted to the demands of second-language teaching. It describes a range of strategies that help to make lessons comprehensible, both by using context that is familiar to students (e.g., building on prior knowledge, providing visual cues) and by adjusting "teacher talk" to their level of language proficiency (e.g., using plain language rather than abstract terminology). This approach may be used in a language classroom or, better yet, in the course of teaching academic subjects. Sheltered instruction enables students to internalize a second language naturally, without conscious effort, purely through understanding messages. Thus direct language instruction, or "skill building," becomes largely unnecessary. So does correction of children's grammatical or pronunciation errors. In fact, such techniques are likely to be counterproductive because they bore students, make them overly self-conscious, and generally make drudgery out of language learning.* In effect, sheltering maximizes comprehensible input in a stimulating, low-anxiety environment, which in turn maximizes acquisition. Rather than "focus on form," students direct their attention to more interesting matters.

Dual immersion adds another rich source of input: the presence of two groups of children learning each other's native language. At an obvious level, they serve as peer tutors for each other simply by interacting socially and academically. More important, to take full advantage of this demographic mix, dual immersion programs must value and validate two different cultures. That is, they must acknowledge and build upon two different foundations of prior knowledge that children bring to school. In doing so, they offer both groups a bicultural experience, an understanding that there is more than one way to make sense of the world. And if reality can be constructed in different ways, the whole concept of education is transformed. It becomes a process of active discovery and evaluation, rather than one of passive reception of official knowledge.

> *We teach a subject not to produce little living libraries on that subject, but rather to get a student to think mathematically, to consider matters as an historian does, to take part in the process of knowledge-getting. Knowing is a process, not a product.*
>
> —Jerome Bruner

A Natural Combination

As it happens, constructivist approaches to learning coincide with the most successful approaches to language teaching. Krashen hypothesizes that second-language acquisition occurs when readers or listeners receive messages just beyond their current level ("$i + 1$," or input plus more), but close enough to make sense in context. With skillful

---

*According to Krashen's theory of second-language acquisition, factors such as anxiety and boredom "raise the *affective filter*"; in other words, they create barriers that keep comprehensible input from getting through.

sheltering to make instruction comprehensible, students can progress to a higher level of proficiency.* While engaged in actual communication, they subconsciously test hypotheses, for example, about the meaning of a new word or grammatical form. Prior understandings (and misunderstandings) give way to new understandings based on the learners' experience. In other words, acquiring a second language is an active process of constructing meaning, not unlike the acquisition of knowledge in other subjects, except that it occurs incidentally, without conscious effort. Krashen's concept of $i + 1$ is analogous to Vygotsky's zone of proximal development, in which scaffolding techniques enable children to reach higher levels of learning.

Constructivism is derived from the recognition that knowledge is constructed rather than absorbed: we form beliefs, build theories, make order. We act on the environment rather than just responding to it—and we do it naturally and continually. It's part of who we are. Learning isn't a matter of acquiring new information and storing it on top of the information we already have. It's a matter of coming across something unexpected, something that can't easily be explained by those theories we've already developed. To resolve that conflict, we have to change what we previously believed. We have to reorganize our way of understanding to accommodate the new reality we've just encountered.

—**Alfie Kohn**

Another connection between constructivism and dual immersion is the role of literacy, a form of meaning-making that extends well beyond the boundaries of the printed page. Reading nourishes— and is nourished by—bilingualism. The more children comprehend what they read in a second language, the more of that language they will acquire.

But their ability to make sense of print in any language depends not only on a grasp of syntax and vocabulary. It also depends on their active engagement with the world around them, which prompts them

---

*Teachers need not worry about precisely aiming for $i + 1$ or introducing grammatical forms in any particular order. As long as they provide sufficient amounts of comprehensible input in the second language, Krashen says, "$i + 1$ will be there."

to construct new knowledge, to build and rebuild conceptual understandings that, in turn, make the written word more meaningful. As the Brazilian educator Paulo Freire once said, "Reading the world always precedes reading the word, and reading the word implies continually reading the world." The same principle applies to the process of becoming bilingual.

It is only natural, then, that dual immersion tends to incorporate constructivist strategies. Indeed, the fact that it does so may help to account for its academic successes, especially for English language learners (a hypothesis that admittedly remains untested by researchers). This is not to say that most dual immersion programs are constructivist by design. Far from it. For teachers in these schools, the label is often unfamiliar or poorly understood. The primary focus tends to be on bilingualism, especially on how the two languages are used for instruction, rather than on questions of educational philosophy. Where dual immersion programs are academically impressive, as many are, the results have usually been attributed to linguistic rather than curricular factors. So their constructivist features tend to be overlooked.

In addition, today's relentless pressures for "accountability" are pushing schools away from student-centered pedagogies and toward rote teaching of material likely to appear on achievement tests. Despite their popularity with parents at the local level, dual immersion programs are not exempt from state and federal mandates that place "high stakes" on test results. Low scores can close a school, derail an educator's career, or keep a student from graduating. It's no wonder that, in many classrooms, test-prep activities have become a substitute for actual teaching, especially for English language learners and other minority children. Even well-established dual immersion programs must now strike a balance between "covering the standards" and fostering language acquisition. So, at times, educators are forced to rely on transmission methods to ensure that students are demonstrating "adequate yearly progress" on tests designed to measure basic skills. Inter-American's creative curriculum had to be suspended for a week or two every spring to prepare students for state-mandated tests.

Despite these obstacles, however, constructivist approaches remain possible where committed educators find spaces in which the excitement of learning can break out. We believe that dual immersion is one of those spaces.

The narratives that follow will offer vivid evidence of why this is so. They illustrate, over the course of a school year, how bilingual instruction was blended with constructivist pedagogy adapted to the needs of second-language learners and how this combination was not only natural but necessary. Rather than isolated vignettes, these are interconnected stories that demonstrate the potential of the best dual immersion schools. They unfold in a second-grade classroom inhabited by teacher Jill Sontag, her eighteen bilingual collaborators, and an unending supply of insects—bugs that crawl, fly, mate, lay eggs, hatch, and die—to the fascination of their human care-givers. To help orient the reader, we begin with a synopsis of the pedagogical principles at work, the fundamentals of dual immersion and constructivism.

❦ CHAPTER TWO ❦

Principles and Practices

> *The notion that all children could and*
> *should be inventors of their own theories,*
> *critics of other people's ideas, analyzers of*
> *evidence, and makers of their own personal*
> *marks on this complex world [is] an idea with*
> *revolutionary implications ... the idea that*
> *every citizen is capable of the kind of*
> *intellectual competence previously*
> *attained by a small minority.*
>
> —Deborah Meier

PHILOSOPHICAL DIFFERENCES IN EDUCATION have a long history. An instructive one, described by Benjamin Franklin, arose in 1744 between British colonists and the Six Nations, a confederation of Iroquois tribes. Treaty negotiators for the colony of Virginia, looking for peaceful ways to assimilate the Indians, had proposed to provide free tuition for several of their youths at the College of William and Mary. The offer was politely declined. According to Franklin, a Six Nations elder explained the tribes' rationale as follows:

> [Y]ou who are wise must know that different nations have different conceptions of things, and you will therefore not take it amiss if our ideas of this kind of education happen not to be the same with yours. We have had some experience of it. Several of our young people were formerly brought up at the colleges of the northern provinces, they

were instructed in all your sciences, but when they came back to us they were bad runners, ignorant of every means of living in the woods, unable to bear either cold or hunger, knew neither how to build a cabin, take a deer, or kill an enemy, spoke our language imperfectly, were, therefore, neither fit for hunters, warriors, or counselors; they were totally good for nothing.

We are not, however, the less obliged by your kind offer, though we decline accepting it, and to show our grateful sense of it, if the gentlemen of Virginia send us a dozen of their sons we will take great care of their education, instruct them in all we know, and make *Men* of them. [Emphasis in original.]

In their pedagogical methods and goals, the Iroquois and the Virginians were worlds apart. Practical, experiential education to serve tribal needs was incompatible with a curriculum of classical erudition for the plantation aristocracy. It's tempting to say the same today about constructivism versus behaviorism, or about multilingualism and multiculturalism versus assimilationism. Each reflects an entirely different vision of what education should be. Yet, in actual practice, philosophical consistency is a rarity in American schools. The vast majority of K–12 educators are intuitive rather than ideological in their professional approach. What results is an eclectic mix of strategies and methodologies, guided by assumptions that are often contradictory.

For example, while some schools celebrate the goal of bilingualism for all, in practice they place a disproportionate emphasis on English for English language learners. Even some dual immersion programs engage in practices, both subtle and obvious, that relegate minority languages to second-class status. English-speaking students may receive lavish accolades for acquiring Spanish while their peers' progress in English acquisition is taken for granted. Often there are class differences between the two language groups that tend to exacerbate such inequities. In some programs Latinos have complained that their children are included primarily to "service" the children of Anglos. It should be noted, however, that at Inter-American and other excellent dual immersion schools, special steps are taken to ensure equal treatment of both languages and active involvement by parents of all ethnicities.

Constructivist and behaviorist practices also coexist awkwardly in many classrooms. Educators may incline toward one or the other, based on factors such as their personal experience of schooling and their professional knowledge about teaching and learning. Problem-solving, scientific inquiry, whole language, collaborative projects, and similar techniques come naturally to some teachers. On the other hand, those who are accustomed to the transmission model may prefer to rely on textbooks, lectures, skill-building exercises, and worksheets—a tendency encouraged by current testing policies. For lack of well-articulated pedagogies, however, most teaching styles today fall somewhere in between.

This lack of clarity and consistency is unfortunate. To replicate successful programs, it's essential to know why they are succeeding; that is, to identify the philosophies, methodologies, and strategies that guide them. The research base on dual immersion and on constructivism remains thin, especially when it comes to controlled, quantitative studies on student outcomes. Yet, thanks to qualitative research, as well as classroom experience over the past three decades, there is much to report about the principles and practices that make these approaches effective.

Dual Immersion

WHILE CONSIDERABLE VARIATION PREVAILS among dual immersion models—for example, in the proportion of languages used—the most successful programs are likely to share these features:

- *Additive bilingualism and biliteracy.* As in one-way, "developmental" bilingual education, dual immersion instruction is organized to ensure that children add a second language without losing their first language or falling behind academically in either language.
- *Mix of language groups.* Students come from a diversity of language backgrounds—including those who are dominant in English, dominant in another language, or bilingual to varying degrees—which provides them ample opportunities to interact with native speakers of the language they are acquiring.
- *Cross-cultural emphasis.* Children acquire an appreciation of different languages and cultures in ways that enable them to develop close relationships across racial and ethnic lines and to construct a positive identity for themselves.

• *Stress on sheltering.* Teachers adjust their language use to students' level of understanding and rely on contextual cues, especially during subject-matter instruction, so as to provide comprehensible input in sufficient quality and quantity to foster second-language acquisition.

• *Language separation.* Lessons are conducted in one language or the other—not in both—although "code-switching" is allowed for students and even for teachers when appropriate; the important thing is to create an environment that enables learners to construct meaning from second-language input in the context of subject-matter instruction.

• *Linguistic balance.* From 50 percent to 90 percent of instruction initially takes place in the lower-status (i.e., minority) language, with the amount diminishing as the students move upward in grade; language arts instruction is provided in both languages, sometimes separately for children in their native language.

• *Classroom resources.* Instructional materials, library books, and research aids are easily available to support student activities in both languages.

• *Long-term approach.* Programs last at least five to six years, since it takes that long, on average, for children to reach grade-level academic norms in a second language; new students are not enrolled in the program after kindergarten or first grade unless they are judged sufficiently bilingual to benefit.

• *Instructional consistency.* Unlike most schools, where students tend to experience a random mix of teaching methods and strategies from year to year, dual immersion ensures consistency not only in program design, but also in educational philosophy, curriculum, and instruction.

• *Assessment.* Locally designed measures of students' academic progress are an integral part of program evaluation and improvement.

• *Personnel quality.* Teachers are well qualified and certified (e.g., in elementary education), fully proficient in at least one of the target languages, and knowledgeable about the theory and practice of second-language pedagogy.

- *Professional collaboration.* Educators meet on a regular basis to plan projects and review curriculum, engage in professional development workshops, solve problems they encounter with individual students or classrooms, address parental concerns, and generally take collective responsibility for student learning.
- *Home-school relations.* Special efforts are made to ensure equitable participation by parents from all ethnic groups; ideally, community and parent representatives play significant roles in school governance.

Constructivist Strategies

UNLIKE DUAL IMMERSION, CONSTRUCTIVISM is, in the words of mathematics educator Catherine Twomey Fosnot, "a theory about learning, not a description of teaching." Thus there is no comparable set of criteria for program design or pedagogical practice. Nevertheless, there are several guiding principles of constructivism with clear implications in the classroom:

- *Goals.* Constructivism defines learning as the development of deep understanding and the ability to think in critical and creative ways. For educators, this means a primary emphasis on concepts—enabling students to construct meaning through reflection and abstraction—rather than teaching "critical thinking" as a preconceived hierarchy of skills or "cultural literacy" through the memorization of officially sanctioned facts. Supports for this type of intellectual exploration include the creative arts, interdisciplinary and project-based activities, and scientific investigations.

> *The pupil's mind is a growing organism. On the one hand, it is not a box to be ruthlessly packed with alien ideas: and, on the other hand, the ordered acquirement of knowledge is the natural food for a developing intelligence.*
>
> **— Alfred North Whitehead**

- *Cognitive development.* True learning is literally a rewiring of the mind, which can only occur through the active engagement of learners in making sense of their experience. Thus, in constructivist classrooms, students not only answer questions and solve problems by testing hypotheses through investigation, experiment, and collaboration with others. They also generate *their own* questions, problems, and hypotheses through open-ended exploration. Knowledge gained through this process transfers across languages, academic disciplines, and home-school contexts.

• *Disequilibrium.* Learning builds on prior knowledge. It occurs when preconceptions are challenged, when mental models are thrown out of equilibrium by unexpected outcomes. This, in turn, inspires learners to restructure their conceptual framework to resolve the contradictions. Student mistakes and misconceptions thus become a valuable raw material used in the making of meaning rather than contaminants to be avoided.

• *Inquiry.* Teachers facilitate the learning process by providing an environment that encourages inquiry and discovery and by supplying the cognitive tools that students may need in their investigations. The latter include "habits of mind" like those developed at New York's Central Park East schools, as described by Deborah Meier:

> the question of evidence, or "How do we know what we know?";
> the question of viewpoint in all its multiplicity, or "Who's speaking?"; the search for connections and pattern, or "What causes what?"; supposition, or "How might things have been different?"; and, finally, why any of it matters, or "Who cares?"

• *Scaffolding.* Teachers help students navigate their own course through the zone of proximal development. To do so, they maximize the use of approaches such as process writing* and the scientific method, which feature step-by-step progressions, and an emphasis on completing projects rather than on performing disconnected tasks.

• *Social interaction.* While learning is a process of meaning-making in the individual mind, it inevitably occurs in a cultural—or multicultural—context. That is, it builds upon one or more foundations of socially constructed meaning, which often prove to be

---

*A series of activities, often in collaborative groups, designed to support the process of composition. The sequence begins with brainstorming or similar strategies, then proceeds to drafting, revising, editing, and finally, publishing.

contradictory. Collaborative learning, especially when it involves children from different languages and cultures, thus provides a stimulating blend of perspectives that can lead to greater understanding. It also places students in the role of teachers.

• *Motivation.* Self-directed learning means exploring what interests the learner—not in a haphazard, chaotic way, but in a purposefully planned community that blurs the line between instructor and instructed. In such classrooms, where everyone participates in the process of discovery, external motivators are rarely necessary. Neither is "behavior management." Encountering new worlds, posing one's own questions, conducting experiments, taking advantage of unanticipated learning opportunities, and working in cooperation with others combine to enhance intellectual self-confidence and feelings of accomplishment. In this context, the internal motivators to learn are far more powerful than the carrots and sticks that fuel the transmission model.

Putting It Together: Curriculum

PRACTICALLY SPEAKING, HOW DOES A THEORY about learning help to shape an educational program like dual immersion? Through the medium of *curriculum.* The term may seem vague and abstract to noneducators, and for good reason. Definitions differ widely.

One approach to curriculum is embodied by the Common Core State Standards—prepackaged lists of knowledge and skills that self-appointed "experts," often with little or no teaching experience, have deemed appropriate for children at each grade level. The standards are accompanied by "performance indicators" that can be easily measured by tests, usually of the multiple-choice variety. In this scheme, curriculum is seen as a way to ensure that all the listed items are "delivered" to students. Hence it must be "aligned" to the standards via textbooks, lesson plans, worksheets, and so forth. Not surprisingly, this view of curriculum encourages teacher-centered pedagogies that stress drill and memorization rather than student exploration and discovery. It assumes that learning is "something done to the learner" by applying external incentives and sanctions. And it calls the end result "achievement."

There are, however, other views of curriculum that are more compatible with constructivist dual immersion programs. One definition, proposed by the scholar William Schubert, describes curriculum as "that which is most worthwhile to know and experience." From this fundamental question, he adds, flow two others: *Why* is it worthwhile? and *How* is it acquired?

Sadly, the answers are often supplied today by government officials rather than by educators or child-development specialists. This is not what Schubert has in mind. He believes that if curriculum is developed at the local level, directly involving classroom teachers, it can be responsive to the needs of communities, families, children, and youth. Teachers in schools guided by a constructivist approach are expected to create—rather than obediently implement—curriculum, and to continually reshape it through interactions with their students.

Of course, teachers must work within the constraints of state and federal policies, and of the institutions in which they teach. Advocacy for consistent curricular and pedagogical approaches thus becomes essential, especially the kinds of advocacy that bring parents on board. This is what happened at Inter-American Magnet School. For example, interviews for prospective teachers were conducted by a panel that included administrators, teachers, and parents, all of whom were knowledgeable supporters of the dual immersion program.

> *The interdependence of the Americas creates a need for individuals fluent in English and Spanish who also have a comprehensive understanding and appreciation of the history, geography, and traditions of the Americas. We believe that the earlier children begin to develop these skills and appreciations, the greater will be their grasp of language and culture. ... The approved Chicago Public Schools curriculum is enhanced by integrating the study of the peoples of the Americas in the areas of art, music, social studies, science, and literature.*
>
> **—Inter-American Magnet School**

There were also times when the Inter-American community saw a need to challenge the Chicago School Board, such as when standardized testing mandates interfered with instruction. A progressive vision of education could not have survived without this kind of activism.

Formal statements of school vision and mission have become commonplace in recent years. Unfortunately, in most cases they serve primarily as window-dressing—noble sentiments designed to prettify business as usual—with little effect on school practices.

Not so at Inter-American, which began with a clearly articulated alternative to traditional education. In addition to the goals of bilingualism and biculturalism, its vision featured "a caring, cooperative, and accepting school climate ... to promote the social, affective, and cognitive development of the whole child, in which the parents are active partners in the formal schooling of their children." From this child-centered philosophy flowed a constructivist approach to pedagogy and a curriculum focused on discovery. The result was a powerful version of bilingual education. What it looked like in practice can be seen in the narratives that follow.

PART II

Narratives

Ms. Sontag's second-grade classroom provides an excellent vantage point for exploring the hows and whys of dual immersion and constructivism. Not that the school, the teacher, or the students could be described as "representative." In many ways they were unique. Also bear in mind that these stories took place in the 1995–96 school year, when Inter-American's faculty, administration, and program differed significantly from those of today. The following narratives, drawn from a year-long research project, simply illustrate what is pedagogically possible. Children's names and a few nonessential details have been changed.

As a public magnet school on Chicago's North Side, Inter-American drew students from all over the city. Who were the children of Room 307? About half came from low-income families; the rest were middle-class. While a majority had Latino roots, many also came from bicultural homes. Their ethnicities were diverse: Mexican, Puerto Rican, Guatemalan, Colombian, Ecuadorian, Belizean, Panamanian, Filipino, Jewish, African-American, and white Anglo-Saxon Protestant. Language backgrounds ranged from English-monolingual to Spanish-dominant to everything in between.

CHAPTER THREE

Welcome to Room 307

*Inter-American influenced my life in a
very good way. When I have kids of my own,
I am not going to send them to a regular
grammar school. If I can't put them in Inter-
American, then I would have to look for another
one with a bilingual setting. That is a given.*

—Inter-American graduate
(Salvadoran female)

AS THE DAY BEGAN, the sounds of English and Spanish swirled and overlapped. Veronica and Alicia lingered in the Reading Corner, where Tupperware bins overflowed with books in both languages. Enrique and César shared a package of Oreos at the Resultados table, while Naomi read them a poem she had written. Other children were coming and going from a small storage area, the "saloncito," as Ms. Sontag handed out paints and poster board. Like other teachers at Inter-American, she was constantly looking for ways to engage her students by encouraging their creative interests.

It was only October, but children's artwork already covered the available wall space, colliding with dinosaur skeletons. Mobiles of geometric shapes, butterflies, and a large paper sun dangled from the ceiling, all crafted by second-grade hands. At the front of the room, a poster headlined "Acciones Valientes" bore the names of Camilo, Amber, and other children who had performed kind and heroic deeds on the playground or elsewhere. Hanging nearby were rosters listing the four cooperative learning groups: *Procedimiento, Pregunta, Resultados,* and *Hipótesis.**

Bilingual lists of synonyms completely filled the rear chalkboard. The words to Gloria Estefan's "Hablemos el Mismo Idioma,"† printed neatly in block letters, occupied a flip chart. Near the classroom door, a sign read, "If I were in charge of the world ..." Posted below, second-grade compositions described a world free of dentists and vegetables and full of chocolate ice cream and people who succeed in life even though they forget to take baths. The teacher's desk, which she never seemed to use, had been taken over by student science projects.

Student creations also spilled into the hallway, which was starting to look like a children's museum, complete with dioramas of prehistoric times and prehistoric predators. A mural spread across an adjacent wall, covered with the imprints of children's feet, illustrating how scientists answer questions about dinosaurs. Responses by each of the learning groups were strategically placed among the footprints.

"¿Cuál dinosaurio corre y cuál camina?" *Which dinosaur runs and which walks?* The Procedimientos had answered: "Los científicos saben que un dinosaurio corre porque hay más distancia entre las piernas del dinosaurio que cuando caminan." *Scientists know that a dinosaur runs because there is more distance between their legs than when they walk.*

Meanwhile, in the main classroom, more art was in production. Student-made big books traveled back and forth between tables. Manny and Amber were painting a poster for the school-wide potluck dinner next week. Dylan worked on the bill of his cap, making designs with a magic marker.

This was the scene in Room 307 when a mysterious visitor arrived.

"Ugggggh!" Veronica shrieked, jumping up from her chair in the Reading Corner. "Lookit, lookit!" Backing away, she pointed at a small black creature making its way slowly across the rug.

Alicia, who had been rummaging casually through the book bins, was startled as well. Peering from behind Veronica's shoulder, she echoed

---

Procedure, Question, Results, and Hypothesis.
†*We Speak the Same Language.*

her friend's sentiment. "Oh, yuck! Gross!"

Soon a cluster of classmates gathered, surrounding the slowly moving object.

"Disgusting!" pronounced Enrique.

"Now our whole room's gonna get disgusting!" Liset wailed.

Amber remained calm. "It's just a bug," she said.

"Yeah, I bet it's a beetle," Manny declared.

"No it's not, it's a water bug," Andy corrected. "I saw one before at my aunt's house, in the basement. They're not poisonous."

"¿Por qué habrá un insecto de agua acá, si no hay agua?" Beatríz was bewildered why there would be a water bug where there was no water. So was Liset. "Is there water leaking in here?" she asked.

From across the room Ms. Sontag observed the commotion and prayed that the intruder was not a cockroach. The dilapidated building should have been replaced many years ago. Cold air crept in through the crevices in the winter, and so did bugs in the fall. But the Board of Education's promise of a new school site never seemed to materialize.

"Hey, I bet if I step on it, it will go cruuuuuunch!" Damion looked at Veronica out of the corner of his eye. But before he could act on his idea, Ms. Sontag arrived.

"Niños, déjenlo en paz," she said. *Leave it in peace, kids.* "Este pobre insecto no ha hecho nada malo a ninguno de ustedes. No es justo." *This poor insect hasn't done you any harm.* "Además es la hora de almorzar. Vámonos." *Besides, it's time for lunch. Let's go.*

Her students slowly trickled toward the door, still wondering what kind of insect the ugly blob could be. And Ms. Sontag, always ready to experiment with curriculum, wondered what she might do with the sudden explosion of interest that had just occurred in her classroom.

Setting the Stage for Discovery

As a practitioner of what she calls "student-centered approaches"—her term for constructivism—Ms. Sontag has consciously designed Room 307 with such principles in mind. The physical environment itself facilitates learning, by stimulating children's natural desire to explore and discover for themselves. Walls decorated with second-graders' creations celebrate their talent and intellect, along with their emerging bilingualism.

The Reading Corner, where children can relax with books in English or Spanish, stresses the importance of literacy. The hallway display with student compositions on dinosaurs emphasizes problem-posing. How and why did scientists come to theorize what we know about dinosaurs? This approach is consistent with constructivist theory, which emphasizes concepts over facts, deep understanding over rote learning, and the transfer of knowledge between disciplines.

Constructivists rely on teaching strategies that inspire further discovery. They believe that active learning is more likely to be internalized, retained, and built upon. That is, it gives memory to what is worthwhile to know and experience.

No Tv Week

"¿EN QUE SEMANA ESTAMOS?" Ms. Sontag asked her eighteen rambunctious charges. *What week is it?*

The children sat on the floor expectantly in two rows, separated by a wide swath of yellow paper running the length of the room. Chairs and desks were pushed toward the north and south walls like useless clutter. Eagerness radiated from eyes, hands, fingers, legs, feet, and torsos. This was not a study in still life.

"Lunes," said Wendell. *Monday.*

"Octubre," volunteered Enrique.

"¿Qué semana?" their teacher persisted. *What week?*

"Halloween!" offered Naomi.

Almost in a whisper, Alicia responded, "Semana sin televisión."

"Otra vez Alicia,"* Ms. Sontag said, with an encouraging smile.

This time Alicia's response was loud and confident: "Semana sin televisión."

"Okay." Ms. Sontag affirmed that this was indeed No Tv Week, as agreed upon by the entire school community. With Inter-American

Once more, Alicia.

parents' approval and support, each student had signed a pledge to turn off the TV set, as well as videos and video games. In this and countless other ways, theirs was hardly a typical public school.

There had been predictable resistance at first. In response, Ms. Sontag read the class a short article discussing how television affects us all— making our brains less active, discouraging exercise, even disturbing our sleep. Also, as a homework project, she assigned the children to count acts of violence in the programs and commercials they normally watched. Everyone was shocked by the results. A discussion about the possible harm from watching so much murder and mayhem convinced the remaining doubters. Besides pledging to boycott TV for the upcoming week, the students agreed to keep a diary describing how alternative projects, games, and get-togethers occupied their time.*

Today's lesson was designed to help them make plans for those activities. "¡Vamos a hacer un mural!" Ms. Sontag announced. *We're going to make a mural!* Continuing in Spanish, she began to organize the work. "¿Quién quiere dibujar una televisión? Dos personas para dibujar la televisión. ¿Quién queremos? ¿Puedes elegir una persona? ¿Quién queremos?"†

Now entering their third year of the dual immersion program, the children were not yet fully bilingual, although their skills varied significantly. When speaking in their second language, most students still made plenty of mistakes. Yet they were usually able to follow what Ms. Sontag was saying. As a former ESL and family literacy teacher, she knew how to make both Spanish and English input comprehensible to second-language learners, skillfully using physical gestures and context, along with a conversational style that stripped her speech of needless complexity. So today, when she asked for nominations, many hands shot up excitedly.

Joaquin was first to be recognized. He recommended Alicia to assist in drawing the television on the class mural. Andy was called on next.

---

*They promised it would be an honest record, recording if and when they succumbed to temptation. As it turned out, not many did. In fact, most students reported not missing TV at all; several commented on how much time they had for other activities.

†*Who wants to draw a television? Two people to draw the television. Whom do we want? Who wants to nominate someone? Whom do we want?*

"¿Quién quiere?"* Ms. Sontag asked. "Yo," he responded. The teacher giggled but accepted his self-nomination.

"¿Quieren elegir a otra persona?" She asked the class for one more candidate.

"José Luis," Leticia suggested.

Following general approval from the class, Ms. Sontag gave instructions to the three designated artists. Continuing in Spanish, she solicited additional volunteers to work on specific parts of the group project, which was intended to highlight alternative things to do in the absence of television. The children responded enthusiastically and bilingually. While English chatter predominated, it didn't entirely muffle the sounds of Spanish. In dual immersion classrooms, lessons take place in one language or the other. But during informal exchanges among students, no formal language policy is enforced.

After repositioning the children to ensure equal coverage of the mural, Ms. Sontag entered the saloncito. As soon as she disappeared around the corner, energetic hands and feet sprang into action. Children leaped over the yellow paper, crawled into and through it, and generally treated it like a pile of autumn leaves.

"C'mon guys, you're messing up. You're messing it up," warned Veronica, ever-concerned about her teacher's approval. "Ms. Sontag is going to get mad at us and she's not going to let us do it." Her words seemed to have little effect on her classmates.

Suddenly, their teacher reappeared with an armload of supplies for painting. "Shhhhhhh... Ya pasó mucho tiempo," she remarked. Much time had passed and the children needed to get to work. But the sight of the art supplies excited them further.

"Niños, no pasaremos nada," Ms. Sontag cautioned. *Children, we won't be passing out anything.* "Si van a jugar, si van a brincar, no les voy a pasar la pintura porque no queremos hacer un desastre." *If you are going to play and jump around, we won't be passing out the paint, because we don't want to create a disaster.* Most of the children calmed down immediately, but a few could not leave the mural paper alone.

"Don't step on it!" Liset cried.

*Whom do you want?

"You're making it dirty!" Beatríz warned.

Several children brought supplies from the saloncito. Soon their eager hands were manipulating paintbrushes, water, and tempera paint.

It was afternoon now, a brilliant autumn day, and the sun was dazzling. The classroom shades were drawn, turning trees into black silhouettes swaying in the wind, as leaves rustled against the windows. Children's voices scattered throughout the room in a turbulent mix of English and Spanish. Again the dominant sounds were English at first, but Ms. Sontag never broke from Spanish. Her students gradually followed suit.

"¡Maestra, maestra! Yo olvidé que ..." Veronica's fractured Spanish was lost in the swirl of noise from her classmates: "¿Cómo ponemos semana sin televisión?" ... "¡Como aquí y allá!"* ... "Yeah! That's a TV!" ... "¡Maestra!" ... "I'll make the TV."

The room itself had come alive with color and motion; it seemed that every space was being used in the service of art. Weaving her way through the chaos, Ms. Sontag commented in encouraging tones on the children's work. "¡Qué bueno!" *How nice!* "¿Qué más tenemos? Leer, jugar, jugar varios juegos. ¿Qué más tenemos?" *What else do we want? Reading, playing different games. What else?*

Marisol was writing, "Ir a cumpleaños" beneath her drawing. "¡Y los cumpleaños!" her teacher exclaimed, chuckling at the talk of birthday parties. At other points on the mural, Wendell was painting a garden plot, while Leticia illustrated a kitchen scene with cookies baking. Naomi worked on a portrait of herself reading a book. Camilo drew himself flying a kite. A few feet away, Manny and Dylan stood together, painting each other's shirts.

With eighteen dedicated artists at work, the mural itself was nearing completion. Finally, it was cleanup time. "Okay niños, es la hora de limpiar," Ms. Sontag announced, giving her students specific instructions on how to proceed. The teacher's voice was like a sudden gust of wind. Children scurried off the floor carrying paint, paintbrushes, and water into the storage room. When they returned, José Luis and Dylan leaped

*Teacher, teacher! I forgot that ... How do we place No Tv Week? ... Like here and there!

joyously over the mural. Amber and Damion tried to follow but landed in the middle of it, amid freshly painted pictures.

"¡Felicidades!" *Congratulations!* The teacher's rebuke was soft yet firm. The room went silent as children stopped to stare at their two classmates sitting in the middle of the freshly painted mural. Their silence seemed to acknowledge a collective responsibility for the mini-disaster. Ms. Sontag needed to say no more.

In a flash they were assisting her, lifting the yellow paper off the floor and above their heads, like a Chinese dragon. Outstretched arms draped it over Ms. Sontag's desk and a series of tables, where it could dry safely before being moved to decorate the hallway. With the mural set aside, all hands were free to reposition chairs and desks, transforming their space back into a classroom.

Outside, the falling leaves spiraled in the cool, crisp air. Inside, the school felt equally rich and colorful.

Collaborative Learning

Today the learning environment is shaped by a project-based activity. What, in another time and place, was a teacher's desk has been transformed into a shared resource, a fitting metaphor for this nontraditional classroom. Meanwhile, movable furniture allows for flexibility; the space can be continually redesigned to foster exploration and experimentation. The teacher still has her own domain separated from the communal area, the saloncito, in which she plans and prepares materials that the students will need.

Ms. Sontag's use of the mural to highlight No Tv Week is also instructive. Murals are relational, a connected series of pictorial elements. Images are not randomly drawn by individuals but collectively created. Children are given the freedom to move about and consult with each other about what they are doing—in either language, although the teacher makes it clear that the language of the lesson is Spanish. In that context, *code-switching* between languages is discouraged, except in a few circumstances, such as when a term needs clarification or the teacher is comforting a child.

When Andy nominates himself for a specific task in creating the mural, Ms. Sontag accepts his offer. Avoiding what would be a small humiliation if she turned him down, the teacher adds a third child to the project. Thus the interpersonal environment of this classroom is characterized by individual freedom and respect, combined with collective responsibility. The children's sense of group ownership becomes evident in the disapproval directed at students who disrupt the project.

A space filled with sound and motion that might appear chaotic to an outside observer is, in reality, guided by constructivist principles.

Clifford Goes to School

THE NEXT MORNING NAOMI made a beeline for the Reading Corner, her favorite part of the classroom, which Ms. Sontag had set aside to encourage students with free time to read books of their own choosing. Bins of Spanish- and English-language volumes lined the shelves. A beanbag chair and two pieces of rug were tossed on the floor beneath.

Naomi was excited about learning to read in two languages at once, especially since some of her cousins were native speakers of Spanish. Leaning against a beanbag chair, she opened the copy of *Clifford y la Tormenta* on her lap, carefully studying the pictures. The English version, *Clifford and the Big Storm,* lay on the floor beside her.

"What book is that?" her friend Marisol inquired, flopping down on the reading rug.

"Shhhhh! Wait!" Naomi didn't look up, as she started to read the Spanish words.

"Let me see," insisted Marisol, who was a stronger reader in Spanish than in English.

"Just wait a minute," Naomi repeated firmly. With Marisol looking over her shoulder, she read silently in Spanish, then turned the page. Furrowing her brow, she gazed for a while at another picture. It featured a vehicle painted with the words "autobús de defensa civil."

Naomi asked what the words meant in English. "It's a bus," Marisol replied matter-of-factly.

"I know that. I want to know what *kind* of bus. I want to *see* that bus. What is it called in English?" Receiving no answer, Naomi picked up the English version and turned to the same page. "Civil defense bus," she announced.

Marisol lost interest and started rummaging through the book bins. She pulled out another bilingual set of Clifford books. After Naomi had finished reading about how the big red dog saved the day during a storm, Marisol showed her *Clifford's First Halloween* and *El Primer Halloween de Clifford.*

"Ohhhhh, let me see that!" Naomi reached for the English version.

"Why don't you, like, read that one to me? And I can read the Spanish one to you," Marisol suggested.

The two girls sat side by side on the reading rug, lounging against the chair. After Marisol read a page of *El Primer Halloween de Clifford* aloud, Naomi would follow with the same page in *Clifford's First Halloween.* Gradually, they made their way to the end, looking intently at the pictures. Soon they were discussing their own costumes for the school's upcoming Halloween parade.

Later that day, after the children had departed, Ms. Sontag gazed in the mirror as she experimented with blacking out one of her teeth. With anticipation, she thought of how the children would react when she came to school on Halloween disguised as a second-grader.

Literacy in Two Languages

Free voluntary reading,* a regular feature of this classroom, provides time for children to read solely for pleasure. Here it takes a bilingual turn. Books are available in each language and sometimes in both. Students choose whatever interests them.

Ms. Sontag has selected separate editions of each story—one in English, the other in Spanish—rather than bilingual editions. The latter are popular, featuring either side-by-side English and Spanish or sequential versions in each language. The difficulty with such formats, however, is that children are likely to read in their stronger language and tune out their weaker one. Of course,

*Also known as sustained silent reading.

one copy of a book is usually cheaper than two. But if the idea is to promote second-language acquisition, providing two separate editions allows the teacher maximum flexibility.

Through her choice of two books, Naomi shows her motivation to learn Spanish. She decides to read in her weaker language, using the English text only as a backup to help her understand unfamiliar vocabulary in Spanish. She also scans the pictures carefully, using the visual cues to enhance her comprehension. Finally, at Marisol's urging, Naomi takes advantage of the social context of her classroom to do bilingual partner reading.

None of this has been directly facilitated by the teacher. Rather, through her choice of books and physical arrangement of the class-room, Ms. Sontag serves as a catalyst for free voluntary reading. The result is to bring together a peer group rich in linguistic resources and an environment in which children feel free to relax and explore enjoyable books.

A Sailor Went to Sea

ARRIVING HOME, NAOMI PULLED A NOTEBOOK out of her backpack and eagerly displayed her homework assignment.

> *Marinero que se fue a la mar, mar, mar,*
> *Para ver que podía ver, ver, ver.*
> *Y el único que pudo ver, y ver, y ver,*
> *Fue el fondo de la mar, mar, mar.**

Her mother, Rebecca, recognized the words. Though not fluent in Spanish herself, she knew they belonged to a hand-clapping game in English that she had played as a child, called "A Sailor Went to Sea." She smiled, as Naomi practiced the game, accompanied by clapping motions, with an invisible partner.

Turning toward her mom, Naomi announced, "This is how people learn Spanish." She recited the lyrics to the song slowly, using English vowel sounds and her version of a Southern accent. She repeated the

---

**A sailor went to sea, sea, sea, / To see what he could see, see, see. / And all that he could see, see, see, / Was the bottom of the sea, sea, sea.*

song three times, gradually speeding up the tempo. With each rendition her speech was slightly less Anglicized. Finally, she said, "He's learning Spanish more," beginning to sing with native-like pronunciation.

Absorbed in the new game, Naomi asked Rebecca to write down the way this fictitious person sang "Marinero." Repeating it slowly in the English-accented version, she stood over her mother's shoulder and watched her compose the transcript.

"Marimero pe se fue ara mar y mar y mar," Naomi dictated, while Rebecca copied down the words from her daughter's notebook. Naomi frowned but continued: "Para ver fer poria very very air." Again, her mother wrote the correct Spanish: "Para ver que podía ver, ver, ver."

Naomi wrinkled her nose. "Mom, give me your pen, please," she said impatiently. Crossing out "que podía," she substituted "fer poria." After a brief pause, she replaced "ver, ver, ver" with "very very air." Naomi surveyed her work and smiled. Then she went back to the first sentence, changed the *n* in "marinero" to an *m* and "a la" to "ara," and added a *y* after "mar." Giggling, she continued to dictate and then revise the Spanish, line by line, until it was thoroughly Anglicized.

"Read it now, mom," Naomi said. Rebecca imitated her daughter's Southern drawl as she read the final transcription:

> *Marimero pe se fue ara mary mary mar,*
> *Para ver fer poria very very air.*
> *Pelo unico kay pudo very very air,*
> *Fue-e el fondo de la mark, mark, mark.*

The verse ended, punctuated by their laughter.

Metalinguistic Awareness

In her wordplay, Naomi displays a heightened sensitivity to language—also known as *metalinguistic awareness*—a common trait among bilingual children, who must constantly compare and contrast different linguistic systems. Not yet fully proficient in Spanish herself, she still enjoys imitating, in spoken and written form, a beginning Spanish learner. According to Ms. Sontag and other second-grade teachers at Inter-American, this behavior was not unusual. The children did not engage in the imitation of English accents with any kind of malicious intent, but rather as a language game—another form of exploring interests outside of school that had been stimulated in the classroom.

Village Builders

SNOW SIFTED SOFTLY DOWN, covering walkways and alleyways behind the school. From the windows of Room 307, children gazed dreamily, adrift in visions of snowmen and snow angels.

"Okay, ¡escuchen bien!" *Listen Up!* Ms. Sontag had to speak especially loud this January morning to get her students' attention. "Atrás están los materiales para el yucayeque." *In the back there are materials for making the village.* She motioned toward multicolored stacks of poster board and construction paper, markers, scissors, tape, glue, pencils, and other assorted supplies. These elements would soon be transformed into a settlement like the ones inhabited by the Taíno people when they first encountered Christopher Columbus.

Making eye contact with the children, now gathered in clusters, Ms. Sontag stressed the importance of working together cooperatively in groups to complete the assignment: "Van a tener que hablar en sus grupos de como van a hacer su parte."

Each group had been given specific responsibilities. For some this meant constructing a *bohío*, or Taíno home; others would create animals or musical instruments used by the Taínos. Enrique, Veronica, and Manny were responsible for both a bohío and the farmland, or *conuco*, laden with major crops of the Caribbean, including yucca, guava, guanábana, and papaya.

The project was part of their school's Curriculum of the Americas, which introduced children to the major cultures that combined to create Latin America: indigenous, Spanish, and African. In second grade the focus was on the Taíno people of Puerto Rico,* and the approach was interdisciplinary, combining social studies with math, science, and the arts. The curriculum was a special passion for Ms. Sontag, who had studied both Spanish and anthropology in college, then lived in Spain for a year.

---

*Other grades studied the Incas, Mayans, Aztecs, ancient peoples of North America, American Indians, and African influence in the Caribbean.

Now she began to orchestrate a total transformation of Room 307. This would no longer be a second-grade classroom; it would be a Taíno village. "Por ejemplo, para las canoas, yo quiero canoas. No quiero *dibujos* de canoas," she declared emphatically. *There would be no drawings of canoes. Rather, there would be canoes!* She motioned toward the art supplies once again. "Van a tener que usar el papel grande y cartón para hacer canoas." The children could use large rolls of wrapping paper and cardboard to create them.

"¿Cómo?" asked a bewildered Beatríz. *How could this be done?*

"No sé, va a tener que hablar con su grupo," Ms. Sontag said. *I don't know; you'll have to discuss it with your group.* She was not going to give explicit instructions or demonstrate. They would have to figure out how to accomplish the task among themselves. And she had every confidence that they would do so without her assistance.

Still, Ms. Sontag was willing to push them gently in a creative direction. "Okay, ¿qué color son las canoas?" she asked Beatríz.

"Café." Beatríz responded that canoes were brown.

"¿Que color va a agarrar para los bohíos?"* The teacher gave her another little push.

"Café claro y café oscuro." Beatríz responded that the houses were light and dark brown.

"¿Y para las hamacas?"

"Café." The hammocks should also be brown.

"¿Y las cotorras?" *What about the parrots?*

"Verde."

"Y rojo," contributed Damion, who thought that green parrots also had some red feathers.

"Sí, rojo también." Ms. Sontag affirmed. "Está bien." *Okay, red as well.* Then she instructed the class: "Quiero que vayan a sus grupos, y quiero que hablen primero, antes de tomar los materiales, para decidir que van a hacer." *Go to your groups and discuss what to do before taking the materials.*

The children had numerous questions about what would happen if they could not fulfill the project requirements.

What color are you going to grab for the houses?

"¿Qué pasa si no hay un color que necesitamos?" Liset wondered. *What happens if we don't have a color that we need?*

"¿Qué pasa si no se puede hacer la casa?" Veronica added with a worried look. *What happens if we can't build the house?*

"¿Cómo que no se puede?" Ms. Sontag replied. "¡Tiene que poder!" *What do you mean you can't do it? You have to do it!*

She refused to micromanage their project. Her hands and arms splayed out to the side, her eyes widened, and her face registered shock. "Por favor, vayan a los grupos." She waved them off to go to their groups and begin the work at hand.

Soon children and projects sprawled across the room, the hum of group activities everywhere. In a corner of the room, Enrique, Veronica, and Manny readied themselves to create a bohío with oversized sheets of wrapping paper. They draped the paper over two stacked chairs and collectively hoisted the chairs onto a table. Then, in a muddle of confusion, construction came to a halt. This bohío left much to be desired.

The three children reassembled in a huddle to brainstorm. They decided that the chairs should be removed. Six small hands began to crinkle the brown paper, flatten it over the table top, and fold it into a large fan. The paper now had both texture and ridges, which the children thought would look more like a rooftop. Manny ran off to find masking tape. When he returned, the paper was taped to one end of the table, one chair was placed back up, and finally the large fan was draped over the top, revealing a Taíno house.

With the bohío in its place, albeit precarious, the children turned their attention to drawing pictures of crops that could be cut out and pasted into the conuco. Conversation began in Spanish and soon turned into a debate on how yucca grow. Enrique believed that they grew on vines. Manny disputed this, pointing out that in the grocery store yucca was sometimes covered in dirt. Veronica agreed that this made a strong case for underground growth, and Enrique was convinced. But they still needed to decide how to draw guava.

"Yo tengo guayabas en mi casa," Manny reported. *I have guavas at my house.*

"Yo sí, pero todavia no los vi crecer." Enrique said he did, too, but hadn't seen them grow.

Although the children had all seen guavas, they apparently did not know if they grew above or below ground. They agreed that the guavas in the grocery store were smooth and clean, unlike the dirty yucca, one indication that they grew above ground on trees. Further evidence for this hypothesis was that guavas were soft, and yucca was hard. In order to grow below ground, a plant would have to be hard enough to withstand the pressure of the earth that it pushed up against.

Veronica volunteered Manny to draw the guavas. "Y tú puedes hacer las guayabas asi,"* she said, demonstrating how she thought it should be done.

"Okay."

"¡Pero yo soy bueno para dibujar guayabas!" Enrique asserted. *But I'm good at drawing guavas!*

"Okay, tú sabes como hacerlos,"† Veronica acknowledged, as if to say "So what?"

But Enrique was determined. "Dámelas," *give them to me,* he said, reaching for the crayons.

The three classmates continued to discuss the project and negotiate how to finish their tasks. Paper rustled as the finishing touches were put on guava trees, the above-ground leaves of yucca, and the corn stalks, each of which was cut and placed on the farmland. But the bohío was still flimsy, and hanging the wrapping paper over a chair to create a roof failed to give it the desired height. So the group decided to string yarn from the top of the paper to the wall. Now the house had height but no depth.

Ms. Sontag strolled by and noticed that the yarn supporting the roof had been taped to a classroom chart. She wondered aloud whether both the chart and the house would eventually fall down.

Veronica listened quietly, her once-animated face now blank. As Ms. Sontag walked away, a fog of confusion descended upon the group members. No one could think of a solution.

By now, cleanup time had arrived and all the other groups had completed their work. The *batey,* or central square, covered the floor in the middle of the room. A Taíno canoe stood near the windows, complete

---

*And you can make the guavas like this.
†Okay, you know how to make them.

with a blue-cloth Caribbean Sea with all sorts of marine life: sardines, crabs, sea turtles, and mahi-mahi. A paper-and-yarn hammock swayed in a corner of the room. The *dujo*, a specially decorated chair, was ready to be placed in the bohío. Musical instruments carefully crafted from cardboard were ready for use. Paper parrots sat in a tree in the Reading Corner. Nearby lay a *buren*, a large Taíno plate on which the ground yucca dough was baked and turned into *casaba*, a kind of bread.

But still there was no house. The group responsible decided they would need to stay in from recess to finish. A tear slid down Veronica's cheek. Skipping recess was not her concern. After all, the students usually seized any opportunity to hang out with Ms. Sontag in their second-grade paradise. It was failure that Veronica found hard to accept.

Suddenly, the group expanded. Alicia and César helped to return the chair to the top of the table. They took large pieces of brown paper and began rolling them up lengthwise and taping each one around the table so that, together, these logs propped up the outer edges of the roof. Camilo taped the bottom of each roll to the floor to secure it in standing position. Leticia, Damion, Joaquin, and Andy joined in. All seven volunteers ended up skipping recess as well.

When the work was finished, a bohío stood complete with walls and a roof. By now it was time to line up for lunch. Only then did the construction crew join Ms. Sontag and their classmates near the classroom door.

Constructing Identity

By exploring the cultural heritage of the Americas, focusing on one culture at each grade level, Inter-American creates a framework for in-depth and meaningful study. Ms. Sontag takes full advantage of the curriculum by turning her second-grade classroom into a Taíno village. Whether figuring out how to construct a bohío, or deciding how yucca and guava grow, the children are encouraged to draw on their prior knowledge and expand upon it, while exploring ideas and gaining confidence in their own creative abilities.

In addition, the constructivist learning environment promotes collaboration and cooperation, not competition. Seven children, on their own initiative, decided to forgo recess until all of their class-mates could join them—quite noteworthy in second grade! More important, they all pitched in to finish the job.

The school's Spanish-English emphasis was the most obvious inspiration for the Curriculum of the Americas, but there are other inherent benefits as well. Language is intertwined with culture, and history is intertwined with the present. Understanding this heritage helps Latino children in particular to figure out where they come from and who they are. But all of Ms. Sontag's students, whatever their ethnic background, benefit by learning about the interconnec-tions between peoples. Time and space to explore other cultures as well as their own enable children to do what no one else can do for them: construct their own identity.

❀ CHAPTER FOUR ❀

The Worms Have Arrived!

*Everything was pretty instinctual learning
Spanish at Inter-American, so I haven't
studied much grammar. I was a really bad
Spanish tutor to people in college because
they would ask, "Well, what is this tense?"
And I'd be like, "Tell me what you are
trying to say and I can say it for you."*

—Inter-American graduate
(white female)

SPRING HAD CREPT BACK SLOWLY, cautiously, after a cruel Midwestern winter. Sun was just beginning to peek through the windows of Room 307. Outside, buds clung to slender stalks while robins pecked tentatively at the soil. Inside, however, there was nothing tentative about this classroom, full to bursting with eighteen pairs of eyes and ears continuing to investigate life.

Worms had taken over Room 307, to the delight of the children. They were everywhere, sleeping in paper cups on tables or burrowing through oatmeal mounds on desktops. Others dangled in midair between seven-year-old fingers or curled up in small palms. A whole jar of the creatures resided in the saloncito, where Ms. Sontag had cut carrots and potatoes into small chunks for their nourishment.

Earlier the teacher had introduced her lesson by asking, "¿Alguna vez has visto un insecto?" After all of the children recalled seeing insects at some point in their lives, she asked them where: "¿Dónde has visto un insecto?" Writing their answers on the board, she helped when necessary to pull out Spanish words and phrases: "En la escuela ... en casa ... en el patio ... en las flores ... en frente de la casa ... por muchas partes ... cerca de una alberca ... en el campo ... en el jardín."*

Ms. Sontag then asked for "el nombre del insecto que has visto," *the name of the insect you have seen.* Again she wrote down the responses: "Abeja ... gusano ... mariposa ... mosquito ..." *Bee ... worm ... butterfly ... mosquito.* Wendell's hand shot up and he was acknowledged. "Un ..." He struggled to find the correct word. "Una ... ant."

"Hormiga," said Ms. Sontag, writing the Spanish word on the board. She added that she, too, knew of an insect, "un gusano de harina," *a meal-worm,* and the students would soon get some of their own.

Now the discussion shifted to the rules for the insects' care. Once more the student responses were posted on the board: "Los miramos en la mesa ... No los pegamos ... Tratarlos bien."†

"Los tratamos bien," *we treat them well,* prompted Ms. Sontag, as she wrote down the revised words, modeling grammatical Spanish. Other children contributed: "No los ponemos en el piso ... No los levantamos ... No nos levantamos."‡

"No vamos a levantar los gusanos así," Ms. Sontag repeated with emphasis. *We won't pick up the worms like this.* "Vamos a dejarlos en la mesa. Y nosotros no vamos a levantarnos." *We'll leave them on the table, and we won't get up from the table.* Then she went to the saloncito and returned with a tray full of cups, each containing oatmeal, two worms, and a small piece of carrot or potato. The children gasped with amazement as she distributed one cup to each child.

"Wow!" Wendell exclaimed.

"Cool!" Joaquin joined in.

"I'm scared!" Veronica announced, with high drama.

"Oooh! Can I play with them?" Camilo asked.

---

*In school ... at home ... on the patio ... on flowers ... in front of the house ... in many places ... near a pond ... in the countryside ... in the garden.

†We look at them on the table ... We don't hit them ... To treat them well.

‡We don't put them on the floor ...We don't pick them up ... We don't get up ourselves.

"Teacher, can we take them out now?" Wendell was getting impatient.

But before Ms. Sontag gave the okay, she led the children in a discussion of the necessary elements of worm care. With the exception of one period each day that was reserved for English, teacher-led activities took place in Spanish. Now the conversation focused on four essential elements needed by the worms for survival: Comida, agua, aire, espacio. *Food, water, air, space.*

Each child then set up a vial in which the worms would be housed, as Ms. Sontag placed a large calendar at the front of the room, marking the day of their arrival. Meanwhile, her students continued to talk excitedly, exchanging observations and speculations about their new charges.

Ms. Sontag strolled over to the Resultados table and placed one worm each into the open palms of Naomi, Enrique, and César. Veronica was too frightened to accept one of her own. But after watching her fellow Resultados staring in awe at their treasures, she changed her mind: "¿Maestra, puedes poner uno en mi mano?"* When the worm touched her hand, however, she screamed, "Ugh!" and dropped it immediately. It landed on a paper on her desk.

"I'm not touching 'em if they get off the paper," Veronica warned the children at her table. "Oooh, they're kissing!" she announced, then walked over to a nearby table to share the news of the romantic activity.

Ms. Sontag distributed magnifying glasses so the children could more carefully examine their new pets. "They kissed, teacher! They kissed!" Enrique shouted with glee, echoing Veronica's suspicion after carefully examining his worms through this scientific instrument. "They kissed two times! They're going to have babies!"

"And then we're gonna have like a hundred worms all over the room," Veronica concluded.

Enrique wrinkled his nose. "I think they did pee-pee on my hand."

"Now I'm really not touching them. Ever!" Veronica was adamant. Yet two days later, she was busily examining one of the creatures as it sprawled across her desk. She stroked it cautiously, then placed a piece

Teacher, can you put one in my hand?

of carrot nearby, tempting the worm to have lunch. Gathering more courage, she plucked a second worm out of the cup and examined it through a magnifying glass with the air of a serious scientist.

Worms were working wonders.

Building on Prior Knowledge

According to constructivist theory, humans have an innate drive to make meaning out of our surroundings and experiences, by constructing and reconstructing mental models of the world. New knowledge is built on a foundation of prior knowledge. So constructivist teachers often initiate instructional activities by reminding students about what they already know—or think they know.

Ms. Sontag begins a thematic unit on insects with this principle in mind. She asks the children if they have seen insects, where they have seen these insects, and what these insects are called. Her questions are posed in Spanish, the second language for many of the students, so the teacher speaks in a way that makes sense in context. In other words, she first builds on their prior knowledge—of the subject and of the language—to ensure that Spanish input is comprehensible and thus conducive to Spanish acquisition. Then she introduces live bugs so that learning can take place in a real-world context: the observation and care of insects.

But What about the Tests?

WHEN VERONICA ARRIVED HOME that afternoon, she glowed as she told her mom, Leah, and her eleven-year-old brother, Antonio, all about the worms. As usual, she spoke to them in English, the primary language of their household. Even though her father came from Puerto Rico and was fluent in Spanish, thus far his children were not.

Veronica explained how cute the worms were, how they ate, slept, and kissed, and how they needed to be cared for. She omitted to mention her initial revulsion.

"That's what you do when you're at school? Play with worms? That's baby stuff," Antonio teased.

"No, it's not. It's hard."

"Yeah, right," Antonio said. "How hard can it be to play with worms? In my class we're studying really hard stuff that's going to be on the test."

"Mommy!" Veronica wailed.

"You're gonna flunk the test! You won't be able to go to third grade!" Antonio never missed an opportunity to taunt his little sister.

"At my school we don't take tests. We have fun. Too bad you can't go there, cuz you don't speak Spanish." Veronica never missed an opportunity to remind her big brother about his own limitations or to brag about her school.

But what she said was at least partly true. Inter-American declined to give her class the Iowa Test of Basic Skills (ITBS), which was optional for second-graders at the time. What's more, it was resisting a mandate from the Chicago Public Schools to administer this standardized test to third-graders as well.

"So who wants to play with worms anyway?" Antonio said. "Hey, what would happen if you cut 'em in half? I bet you'd get two worms. Veronica, do you want me to bring a knife to your school and cut 'em in half? I'll do it for you!" This was the most excitement he had ever shown about his sister's classroom.

Veronica's face registered horror. "You are supposed to take care of them, not kill them! Mommy, he can't ..."

"Don't worry, baby, he's not going to your school."

The first lesson on worms had been a success.

A Constructivist View of Assessment

Assessment takes a different form in Veronica's school than in Antonio's. At Inter-American, testing is just one type of information used to improve curriculum and instruction. In 1992, at an assembly of more than seventy-five parents, teachers, administrators, and community members, the school adopted a firm policy of limiting standardized tests. In line with its "philosophy of educating the whole child," the school resolved to evaluate "progress not only in knowledge, but in skills and abilities such as thinking, valuing, and social participation. The data for evaluating comes from a variety of sources, not only paper-and-pencil assessments, but observations of what students do outside as well as inside the classroom."

While standardized tests like the ITBS were administered after the third grade, they were considered merely one form of evidence, offering useful—but only partial—evidence about student learning. After all, how could a multiple-choice test fairly and accurately evaluate the knowledge construction going on in Room 307, as children interacted with worms? Inter-American recognized a pitfall that many other schools have since experienced: Unless kept in perspective, standardized testing can restrict—and even shape—curriculum and instruction.

Marisol and Jessica

ANTICIPATION ROSE HIGHER with each book that Ms. Sontag held up while reading the titles and authors aloud. When she placed a pile of books on each table, the children were barely able to restrain themselves.

A few dived into the stacks as if they were jumping into a cool lake on a hot day. But the rules were clear. Each time the teacher called out "pass," the girls and boys had to exchange books. When everyone at the table had reviewed each book, Ms. Sontag moved the piles to different tables, giving everyone the same opportunity. After she distributed a list of available titles, students indicated their order of reading preferences. Excited chatter filled the room.

"¿Cuál es tu favorito?" Joaquin asked Alicia. *Which is your favorite?*
"Spider Kane and the Mystery under the May-Apple," she replied.
Wendell told his tablemates, "I hope I get the one about the ugly bug!"
"Tonight I'm gonna sit down and put them in groups based on who likes what," Ms. Sontag announced. "So tomorrow we should be able to organize our reading groups. Okay?" She spoke in English, since this exchange took place during a lesson in English language arts.

Next came "Yo Leo,"* the portion of the day when Ms. Sontag read aloud to the children in English or Spanish. Today she started on *Chocolate Covered Ants,* a book by Stephen Manes. She was a dramatic reader

---

I read.

and easily captured the attention of her second-graders. A collective cry of "Awwww!" went up when the first chapter ended. But science was next, and there was no time for disappointment.

"Gusanos with chocolate!" Andy declared, heralding the return of the worms.

"With whipped cream on top!" shouted Manny.

Ms. Sontag wished them "¡Buen provecho!"* and then proceeded with the lesson. On a large piece of chart paper, she printed the heading "Vocabulario de Insectos" and, beneath it, "gusanos de harina," the Spanish for *mealworms*. She asked the children what they thought they knew about them.

"No tienen pelo," Dylan said, volunteering that they had no hair. This became the first item on the list. Ms. Sontag expanded on this theme, along with other features of the bugs' appearance. After some discussion, "Esqueletos están afuera" was added to the chart. *Skeletons are on the outside.* Then she asked the children how many parts of an insect they could name.

A small chorus of voices responded, some reverting to English. In Spanish, Ms. Sontag reminded the class that, when they spoke about "gusanos de harina," they were to speak in Spanish. Then, without missing a beat, she continued. The list on the chart grew as children began to contribute insect-related vocabulary: "Secciones ... cola ... boca." *Sections ... tail ... mouth.*

Dylan noted that "las bocas son como están aquí." He pointed below his mouth, toward his chin. "Están como ... abajo."†

"Bocas debajo de la cabeza," Ms. Sontag added to the list. *Mouths below the head.*

Dylan had more to say. "Son como una ... ese ..." He bent over from the waist, demonstrating the concept for which he lacked Spanish vocabulary. "No son como nosotros porque ..." This time he cupped his hand so that it resembled the shape of a partially curled mealworm. "Están así." Then he stood erect. "Y nosotros así."‡ Like other English-

---

Good appetite!

†*Their mouths are like this here. They are like ... below.*

‡*They are like a ... this ... They are not like us because ... They are like this. ... And we are like this.*

dominant children, Dylan sometimes found it helpful to act out what he was trying to say in Spanish.

Ms. Sontag clarified the concept that he was dramatizing. "Aaaah, los gusanos de harina se doblan, son flexibles." *The mealworms bend, they are flexible.*

Dylan nodded his confirmation and Ms. Sontag wrote "Doblan" on the board. Now the discussion became animated, as other children chimed in:

"Ojos pequeños como sal." *Small eyes like salt.*

"Son cafés." *They are brown.*

"Son chiquitos." *They are very small.*

"Seis patas." *Six paws.*

After compiling an exhaustive list, Ms. Sontag asked for the last time if there was anything else to say about the worms: "¿Otra cosa sobre gusanos?"

"Son gusanos," Dylan offered, with an air of finality. *They are worms.*

"Sí, son gusanos," Ms. Sontag confirmed, a twinkle in her eye.

Next, each child received a calendar and a data-collection sheet as Ms. Sontag explained their usage. On the calendar they were to note the arrival date of their mealworms. On the data-collection sheet they were to draw the creatures as realistically as possible, using the magnifying glasses as scientific tools to guide them, then to write down any significant observations.

Naomi began taking oatmeal out of her cup and sprinkling it in a geometric pattern on the paper surrounding the worms. Marisol looked on from the next table. Acknowledging her gaze, Naomi proudly announced, "This one is named Marisol." Her friend grinned with pleasure to be so honored.

Passing by Naomi's table, Ms. Sontag inquired about the name of the other worm, who might feel bad if left nameless. "¿Y cómo se llama el otro? Va a sentirse mal si no tiene un nombre y su compañero sí."

"Jessica," Naomi replied without hesitation. Carefully, she replaced the mealworms and the oatmeal back into the cup. The teacher asked how she could tell them apart. "Marisol is the one with the red tail and Jessica sleeps a lot." In a few moments Naomi was making a house for her worms using two pieces of paper, with the top sheet cleverly folded to form a roof.

"Mira la casa," Naomi told Veronica. *Look at the house.* But before she could place Marisol and Jessica inside their new home, it was time to clean up and share observations with the class. Naomi had been so involved in Jessica and Marisol's housing situation that she had left her paper blank. Hurriedly she wrote, "Duermen mucho y comen mucho." *They sleep a lot and they eat a lot.*

Scientific observations were shared and then interpreted through the medium of clay as the children began an art project. A Selena tape played in the background, while small artists gave form to brightly colored fantasy worms. Veronica sang to the music, moving her hips from side to side as she scooped up chunks of clay and fashioned them into eyes and legs. Andy and José Luis danced in the back of the room, while the mealworms slumbered in their oatmeal beds, undisturbed by the pulsating Tex-Mex sounds.

Literacy and Scaffolding

Ms. Sontag encourages reading in multiple ways. Free voluntary reading and partner reading, as well as her own oral interpretations, foster a love of literature. Reading groups are organized by interest rather than reading level. In addition, by thematically connecting the classroom selection of children's literature to current investigations and then to an art project, interdisciplinary study occurs on the second-grade level.

She scaffolds language and subject matter in multiple ways as well. Tapping into the children's prior knowledge of insects helps to develop science vocabulary. Data-collection sheets and calendars add visual interest, as do the children's own insect pictures. Handling live bugs and constructing clay models add kinesthetic support. Meanwhile, Spanish is reinforced through teacher modeling and persistence, as well as skillful sheltering to make the lesson comprehensible for second-language learners.

A Lullaby for Worms

It had been a hard week, and Leah was weary from the combined responsibilities of working and parenting. Nonetheless, she took her children for their six-month dental checkup. Waiting in the reception area, Veronica became excited by a toy. From a wooden base, parallel wires climbed up, down, and around, like the tracks of intertwined roller coasters holding brightly colored beads. Veronica ran over to play, exclaiming, "They're gonna go like gusanos!" She tried to entice her mother to play "worms," but Leah was preoccupied with getting home and serving dinner in time to attend the Local School Council meeting at Inter-American that evening.

So Veronica turned to her brother, just emerging from his checkup. "C'mon Antonio, play gusanos with me," she said sweetly.

"That's baby stuff." Antonio was dismissive as usual.

"No it's not. My teacher looooves gusanos."

Leah was already heading toward the door. "If you want to eat dinner, we have to get going. I have to get to my meeting and I can't be late. Tonight we're planning the next Noche Cultural."

Veronica grinned slyly. *Cultural Nights* were special events at Inter-American designed to help parents and children learn Spanish. "Uh-oh, we better hurry," she agreed. Then she rolled her eyes in Antonio's direction. "We need to take Antonio to *all* of the Noches Culturales, so he can learn Spanish."

She continued: "Qué vergüenza que Antonio está en el sexto grado pero puede hablar solamente en inglés. Piensa que es tan inteligente, pues no es." *What a shame that Antonio is in sixth grade, but he can only speak English. He thinks he so smart but he really isn't.*

Antonio stewed. "Mom, make her stop talking in Spanish," he pleaded. "It's not fair!"

Later that evening Leah returned home, determined to get eight hours of rest. Believing her children were already asleep, she climbed into bed. But as her eyes closed and the world began to drift away, she heard the familiar sound of soft footsteps. Veronica had come to say goodnight. She kissed her mother's face, then nestled beside her, her fingers combing through Leah's hair, singing the lullaby she had just composed about worms.

Nuestros gusanos
son bonitos,
son bonitos,
son bonitos.

Nuestros gusanos
son chiquitos,
son chiquitos,
son chiquitos.

Nuestros gusanos
son rojo café,
son rojo café,
son rojo café.

Nuestros gusanos
duermen mucho,
duermen mucho,
*duermen mucho.**

The Home-School Connection

When children are engaged in the classroom, what they learn will emerge naturally outside of school, and a powerful home-school connection becomes possible. As educators and parents work together to encourage learning in many contexts, the school's vision becomes a reality—not just words on paper.

Leah understands that a strong partnership with Veronica's teachers can help to strengthen her daughter's bilingual and bicultural development. For this reason she ran for and was elected to a seat on Inter-American's Local School Council,† which sponsored numerous school functions that involved parents and community.

---

*Our worms are pretty; our worms are tiny; our worms are red brown; our worms sleep a lot.

†Local School Councils (LSCs) were part of Chicago's sweeping school reforms of the late 1980s. Composed of ten elected representatives—six parents, two teachers, and two community residents—along with the school principal, the council became the governing board of every public school, charged with making essential decisions, such as approving the budget and selecting the principal. LSCs have had a mixed impact, sometimes marred by political squabbles and factional in-fighting that have undermined instructional programs. Yet there were also some brilliant successes, as exemplified by Inter-American, where a nontraditional program was empowered to flourish in part because of the LSC's advocacy and in part because of the school's history of local control and parent-teacher partnerships.

Noches Culturales were especially helpful for English-dominant parents as they tried to help their children navigate a bilingual curriculum. Families sang songs and played games together in Spanish. Teachers distributed resources, such as lists of common vocabulary for parents to keep and use at home, while Latino artists provided entertainment. A variety of tasty food was always available. Another popular event was the annual Young Authors Celebration, which recognized up to three hundred children and featured a guest speaker from the community. The Pan-American assembly and the Taste of Inter-American, which swelled the school with families and staff, were yearly staples. Other activities, such as Science Night and the Algebra Workshop varied from year to year.

In addition, parents were seen in classrooms on a daily basis. They assisted teachers, contributed to instructional activities, and were always free to observe. The sense of community at Inter-American was tangible. It could be heard, seen, tasted, and felt.

❦ CHAPTER FIVE ❦

Nincas and Ninfas

*Inter-American literally made me the
person I am today—open-minded and
eager to learn about other cultures.*

—Inter-American graduate
(African-American male)

Ms. Sontag opened the door and entered the silent classroom, where a package of insect eggs had arrived in the school mail. She smiled. Her students were away in the library, so she had almost forty minutes to prepare for class. With excited fingers, she unwrapped the brown cardboard carton and went to work.

The mealworms lay on a table nearby in small vials. They had molted and were no longer fun to play with. Their dry, crumbly skins rested atop mounds of oatmeal in plastic cups. A chart at the front of the room noted the changes that had occurred: "Café, blanco" ... "café claro" ... "se pusieron blancos" ... "su piel está saliendo" ... "hay cáscara en el vaso."* The onetime classroom pets, now motionless, had lost their hold on second-grade attention. But Ms. Sontag had other plans.

The sounds of bouncing feet and hallway chatter soon ended her reverie of bugs. Children spilled into the classroom, eager for whatever activities the afternoon would bring. Ms. Sontag was ready. She explained,

---

Brown, white ... light brown ... they turned white ... their skin is falling off ... there is a shell in the cup.

in Spanish, that they would receive new insects and that each group would be responsible for their care. Then she distributed vials containing brightly colored specks. Children gazed in fascination at the vivid blend of orange, yellow, and pink, enmeshed in wisps of bleached cotton.

Wendell ventured the first guess. "Oh! They're ants!"

"I know what they are," said Veronica.

"¡Arañas!" Manny shouted. *Spiders!*

"Spider webs!" declared Dylan, building on his friend's idea.

From across the room Andy cried out, "Lice! They're lice! They're lice! They're lice." Although his father was Mexican-American, Andy's Spanish remained limited.

"¡Yo sé, yo sé! ¡Piojos!" Enrique shouted, supplying the correct word. Soon a bilingual chorus took up the idea of head lice.

Ms. Sontag formalized the guessing session by asking for a show of hands from those who thought they knew what the jars contained. Each child who volunteered an answer was asked to explain the theory behind the conclusion. When it was Veronica's turn, César leaned toward her to whisper a reminder of their table's consensus.

"Que son arañas ..." *That they are spiders.*

"Arañas," Veronica spoke out loud and clear.

"¿Y por qué crees que son arañas?" Ms. Sontag pressed. *And why do you think they are spiders?*

"Porque los arañas tienen como ... Yo no sé cómo decirlo."* She moved her hands to construct an imaginary spider's web, then pointed to the vial on her table as a substitute for the idea she could not express in words.

"Do you know how to say it in English?" César whispered to her. "Like a web."

"Telaraña," Ms. Sontag coached. *Spider's web.*

The child continued. "Y ... y hay una chiquita, hay una chiquita que se puede verlo ... verlo ... muy chiquito ... y ver como hay unas arañitas."†

"Aaaaaaah," Ms. Sontag signaled her comprehension. Veronica must have thought the wispy cotton in the vial was a spider's web.

Because spiders have, like ... I don't know how to say it.

†*And... and there is a little one, there is a little one that you can see it ... see it ... very little ... and see how there are little spiders.*

The hypotheses continued. Joaquin mentioned "huevos" as one possibility. A number of his classmates elaborated on what type of insect eggs they might be. When group curiosity reached its peak, Ms. Sontag announced, "Estos son huevos pero todavía no sabemos de que son. ¿Verdad? So, vamos a esperar, vamos a ver si cambian, y a qué cambian." *They are eggs, but what kind? Let's wait and see what changes occur.*

Indeed, the promise of change lies everywhere in this room. Change in the mealworms asleep in their molting. Change inside the mysterious orange-yellow-pink eggs nestled in their cotton wisps. Change in the searching, reaching, grasping for new words—for ways of describing the ever-evolving world of Room 307.

Integrating Language, Content, and Process

In dual immersion classrooms, a second language and subject matter are taught simultaneously. In constructivist classrooms, subject matter and process are taught simultaneously. Thus, in a constructivist dual immersion classroom, all three—language, subject matter, and process—are integrated. None of this happens by accident. Rather, it begins with the teacher's choice of how to present the material.

In this case, the subject matter is insect study, the language is Spanish, and the process is discovery learning. Ms. Sontag understands the importance of using real-life creatures, contextualizing lessons in a way that simultaneously promotes second-language, academic, and cognitive development.

This approach differs markedly from the transmission model. Rather than lecturing the children on "what they need to know" about insects—the Common Core approach—Ms. Sontag invites them to speculate about the contents of the vials, then to investigate in the days ahead what they actually contain. In other words, she encourages them to generate hypotheses, test them on the basis of observations, and come to conclusions about insects. In effect, this process-based approach introduces the concept of scientific inquiry. Answers are not given; children are instead encouraged to discover them on their own.

Little Cotton

NAOMI STUDIED THE VIAL with a blank stare. The brightly colored eggs had disappeared, leaving in their place minuscule black insects that were crawling through the cotton. Putting the vial down, she pulled out a pink marker and began to draw idly on a paper in her lap.

A few minutes later Ms. Sontag refocused the attention of the class to discuss their observations and reach a few conclusions. She began by reminding the children what they had previously learned about worms: "¿Cúales son las cuatro cosas que un animal o un insecto necesita para sobrevivir?" *What are the four things that an animal or insect needs to survive?*

Naomi's hand shot up. Her response, "espacio," *space,* was written down as the first requirement for survival. When complete, the list included "aire," "comida," and "agua." *Air, food, water.*

Ms. Sontag demonstrated how to construct a habitat for the small black bugs, giving each group the responsibility for setting one up at its table. Naomi put the paper and marker back into her desk and joined the group effort, interacting in Spanish with the other members of the Resultados.

As the afternoon wore on, however, the children's conversation became bilingual or English-dominant. César made a "tree" out of the twigs the children had collected at recess, and Naomi spread stretched-out cotton balls in its branches, punching holes in the Ziploc bag for air. Enrique cracked the sunflower seeds out of their shells with his teeth while Veronica set up the water source.

"¡Apúrate!"* Veronica rushed Enrique along as he crunched down on a seed and then devoured it, despite Ms. Sontag's caution against eating them raw. The group needed twenty-five shelled seeds, but the pile was growing at a snail's pace.

Veronica wrinkled her nose as she held up the vial of black bugs. "Who wants to put them in?" she asked.

Luckily, Naomi and César did not share her squeamishness. Like surgeons performing a delicate operation, they moved the black bugs into their new home. Naomi held open the bag as César opened the vial and

Hurry!

placed it inside the Ziploc habitat. Finally, as Veronica looked on from a distance, César sealed the bag, Naomi labeled it with the Resultados name, and they carried it to the front of the room.

With four plastic bags taped to the front board, Ms. Sontag conducted the final bug discussion for the day. The children learned that the insects they were studying were called "insectos de algodoncillo," *milkweed bugs,* and that in their current stage of development they were called "ninfas," *nymphs.*

"¿Qué quiere decir *ninfa*?"* Ms. Sontag did a comprehension check on the meaning of the word.

"¡Bebé!" the children exclaimed. "¡Bebé algodoncillo!"

"Yo sé," volunteered Naomi. "Algodón pequeño." Since insecto de agodoncillo is derived from the word *algodón*—cotton—she reasoned that the young insect would be referred to as a "little cotton."

"Bien pensado, Naomi," said Ms. Sontag. "Pero eso significa algo diferente." *Good thinking, but that means something else.*

She continued: "De lo que estamos hablando es del momento en la vida del insecto de algodoncillo que viene después de que sale del huevo." *What we are talking about is this stage in the life of a milkweed bug, the stage that comes after the egg is hatched.* "La ninfa."

"Ninfa," repeated Alicia.

"Ninfa," echoed several classmates.

"Ninca!" Amber gleefully shouted an invented word.

"¡Finca!"† responded Manny.

"¡Fincas!" Dylan and Andy chimed in.

Amid giggles, several children began to chant: "Nincas! ... ¡Fincas! ... ¡Incas!"

"No, no, no son Incas. Queremos tener respeto," cautioned Ms. Sontag . "Son ninfas."‡

"¡Ninfas!" the girls and boys shouted.

At her seat Naomi played with the word *ninfa* as she had previously played with her paper and marker. "Ninfa ... ninca ... finca ... ninfa."

What does ninfa *mean?*

†*Farm!*

‡*No, no, they are not Incas. We want to be respectful. They are nymphs.*

Classroom activity resumed as calendars were updated and observations were recorded. Ninfas crawled around in plastic bags taped to the front board while children carefully inscribed "ninfa" on their charts.

"Vamos a ver qué pasa con los insectos de algodoncillos," Ms. Sontag reminded them. *We are going to see what happens with these milkweed bugs.* Change had now occurred, yet still the class waited to see what would happen next.

Developing Vocabulary in Spanish

Vocabulary development is paramount in opening up academic subjects for the learner. It is especially important when subjects are introduced in a second language, since students cannot always depend on contextual clues to help them decipher the meaning of words. Here Ms. Sontag maximizes the problem-solving potential of the insect curriculum to motivate the children to expand their Spanish vocabulary. They understand that, based on their scientific inquiry, they will engage in formal discussions and written documentation of the life cycle of insects. And to do so, they will need the appropriate words.

When tied to inquiry and an interesting context, vocabulary development can be fun. The students seize the opportunity to engage in Spanish wordplay, using the word *ninfa* as their base and moving to *ninca* (a nonsense word using Spanish phonetics), *finca*, and *Inca*. Spanish vocabulary, the key to opening the world of insects in Room 307, is reinforced while reading skills are enhanced as the children play with sounds and words. In this way, academics and Spanish literacy are authentically interwoven.

Bug Bets

"Wow, wow! Wow, wow, wow!" Manny's face beamed in amazement. Smiling broadly, he held up the small vial and examined it. Inside, a winged insect crawled lazily around its prison. "It's a lightning bug," he proclaimed.

"See, it's not a butterfly," responded José Luis, another member of the Preguntas.

"We made a bet and you owe me a dollar!" Andy cried triumphantly.

"Yeah," Manny conceded. "It didn't turn into a butterfly."

Nearby, the Resultados were more subdued. Naomi examined her vial carefully. She was not so easily impressed. "He's eating the oatmeal," she finally concluded, forgetting that in its past life the bug had been named Jessica or Marisol.

As the children continued their quiet examination, Veronica replaced the cap on her vial. "I don't want to touch his air," she explained. César and Naomi raised their eyebrows quizzically. After deciding to inspect each other's bugs, the Resultados passed their vials around the table. Veronica was disappointed with her specimen. "¡Maestra, mío no está haciendo nada," she complained. *Mine isn't doing anything.*

Ms. Sontag knelt beside the Resultados table. Enrique, his face glowing brightly, held up a vial. Everyone could see his winged bug moving as rapidly as the constricted space would allow. Veronica abandoned her own insect and giggled wildly as she looked at Enrique's. Soon clusters of children from other tables were gazing at the frantic bug. Damion was gazing at Veronica, who ignored him as usual.

"He's doing exercises!" Veronica shouted, leaping out of her chair and demonstrating. With renewed enthusiasm, she returned to look inside her own vial and was excited to see her bug coming slowly to life. "Lookit, he's turning!" she shrieked dramatically. César joined her dance routine and the two bounced over to visit the Preguntas and their insect collection.

"Veronica y César … A su mesa." Ms. Sontag told them to return to their table. It was time for the students to discuss their observations. "A ver, ¿un cambio?" *Had they observed a change?*

Several noted that the mealworms had, in fact, changed. There was some speculation as to what the new creature might be. Manny stuck to his idea of a lightning bug. One of the most bilingual students in the classroom, he still lacked this bit of vocabulary, which his teacher supplied: "una luciérnaga." However, this was no lighting bug. None of the other children could guess its identity, either. The mystery was finally solved when Ms. Sontag wrote the word *escarabajo* on the board. "Maestra, ¿que son en inglés?" Naomi inquired. *What are they in English?*

Next to escarabajo Ms. Sontag wrote "beetle." Then she directed the children's attention back to the chart labeled "Cambios," *Changes.*

Beneath their previously recorded observations, the class decided to add the sentence, "Hay un escarabajo." *There is a beetle.*

The teacher now steered the discussion to a consideration of the overall changes that had transpired.

"Entonces, niños, tenemos escarabajos, pero cuándo empezamos, ¿qué tuvimos, qué tipo de insecto tuvimos?" she asked. *So now we have beetles. But when we began, what type of insect did we have?*

"Gusanos de harina," the children responded in unison.

"Gusanos de harina," Ms. Sontag repeated. "Luego cambiaron, ¿a qué? ¿Quién se acuerda?" *Who remembers what they changed into?*

"Crisálida."

"Crisálida," repeated the teacher. *Chrysalis.* "Y ahora tenemos ..." *And now we have ...*

"¡Escarabajos!" the children responded.

"Vamos a considerar el gusano de harina como el bebé. La crisálida es como el adolescente. Luego, el escarabajo es el ..." *Let's think of the mealworm as the baby and the chrysalis as a teenager. So the beetle is what?*

"Mamá o papá," suggested José Luis. *Mom or dad.*

"Mamá o papá o, ¿qué es otra palabra para una persona grande?" *What is another word for a big person?*

"Madre o padre," responded Joaquin. *Mother or father.*

"Adulto," volunteered Marisol.

"¡Adulto!" Ms. Sontag echoed with enthusiasm as she wrote down the word. After an extended conversation, it was time to mark the latest development on individual calendars. The words *crisalida, gusano de harina, escarabajo,* and *adulto,* joined the never-to-be-forgotten *ninfa* on charts throughout the room.

Cleanup was swift; it was time for lunch. One of the children asked Ms. Sontag what was on the menu.

"Un escarabajo para el almuerzo," she replied, "con un poquito de chocolate!" *A beetle for lunch ... with a little bit of chocolate.*

Comprehensible Input

Another insect transformation has occurred in Room 307 and the children have various theories about its meaning. Ms. Sontag's sheltered use of Spanish helps them understand what has happened. She is able to provide comprehensible input, language that is made accessible by using it in real-life situations that are meaningful to the learner. Context is on her side, by design rather than by accident.

The children are not only talking about insects; they are witnessing live ones changing before their very eyes. Hands-on observations have led to authentic theorizing about what the emergent bugs might be. Motivation is high and the children are primed for discovery. Ms. Sontag uses plain, uncomplicated language and converses with the students, one phrase at a time, to be sure they understand before she moves on to the next idea. The classroom insect chart serves as a visual support to the discussion.

Never missing an opportunity to motivate her young charges to understand the target language, Ms. Sontag ends the session on a humorous note, made possible by previously shared readings about chocolate-covered ants and Andy's joke about gusanos as candy.

Rock-Eggs

AMBER AND ANDY, TWO ENGLISH-DOMINANT children, sat on the rug in the Reading Corner. A Spanish-dominant classmate, Alicia, lay on her back, her head resting on the sofa cushion. She read a page in English from *Spider Kane and the Mystery at Jumbo Nightcrawlers,* as Amber and Andy listened and followed along in their own copies of the book. They alternated between reading and listening, sandwiching in a few private jokes and giggles as well.

On the back wall, a calendar hung on a corkboard strip. String was draped from its outer edges, with clothespins holding each Ziploc habitat for the insectos de algodoncillo. Ms. Sontag signaled it was time for the children to close their books and return to their desks. "Tengo algunos insectos nuevos para ustedes." *I have some new insects for you.*

As Ms. Sontag spoke, Veronica braided her hair. One braid was already complete. She gathered the rest of her hair and separated it into three strands.

The teacher set a new vial down in the middle of the table. Veronica picked it up, studied it with a serious air, and then contemptuously put it back down. "They're rocks and I don't like 'em," she declared. Then she chewed on the end of the freshly made braid. It was true; the tiny eggs did resemble fragments of pebbles, gray and aesthetically unappealing.

Ms. Sontag passed out magnifying glasses to each child. Naomi turned toward Veronica, opened her mouth wide and bared her teeth. With her instrument Veronica inspected Naomi's teeth. The girls giggled. Veronica twisted one of her braids below her own chin where she could examine it under the magnifying glass. César and Enrique drew pictures. The rock-eggs sat in the vial in the middle of the table, unnoticed.

Ms. Sontag facilitated a guessing session about what the rock-eggs might be. She listed the children's ideas on the board: *Piojos, huevos, orugas, hormigas.** "Grasshoppers," Wendell added.

"¿Cómo?" Ms. Sontag answered. Joaquin volunteered the translation: "Chapulínes." The teacher printed the word on the board, noting that "saltamontes" could also be used. "Moscas" was offered softly, but was not recorded; nor was "rocas."†

Ms. Sontag distributed labels for group names to be stuck on the vials. Veronica began to place the Resultados label on the side, but the teacher instructed her to put it on the top instead. César noticed that there were no holes in the cover. "¿Por qué no necesitan aire?" he wondered. *Why don't they need air?*

Naomi knew why. "Porque son huevos," she said. *Because they are eggs.*

Ms. Sontag nodded, then directed the attention of the class to the calendar at the back of the room, and the arrival of the new batch of eggs was noted.

While the rest of the girls and boys finished marking their vials, César, Enrique, Veronica, and Naomi began to sing:

*Lice, eggs, caterpillars, ants.
†Flies, rocks.

La cucaracha, la cucaracha,
Ya no puede caminar,
Porque no tiene, porque le falta,
*Las dos patitas de atrás.**

The Teacher as Facilitator

Worms are so much more exciting than "rock-eggs." So what happens when students just aren't interested? In a traditional classroom the teacher might turn to "classroom management"—a euphemism for controlling student behavior through rewards and punishments—based on the assumption that students are at fault when they fail to pay attention, refuse to cooperate, or otherwise act out. In constructivist classrooms, by contrast, the emphasis is not on control but on student engagement. When activities are relevant and purposeful to children, discipline in the traditional sense is rarely an issue. Of course, not every activity will engage every child. Yet, if mutual respect and love of learning are regular features of the classroom, temporary lulls will not be disruptive.

Ms. Sontag approaches this problem from a constructivist point of view. Undaunted by some children's lack of interest in today's lesson, she does not force anyone to focus on the insect eggs. Nor does she diminish the rapport she enjoys with her students through countless reminders to pay attention. Instead, she turns the lesson into a guessing game, followed by a physical task: preparation of the future insect habitat. Patience is necessary for deep learning to occur. Besides, who is to say that one cannot braid hair and also pay attention?

Everyone Eats Insects

THE NEWLY ARRIVED CATERPILLARS had spun their silk, attached themselves to twigs, and shed their skins over the weekend. Sadly, the changes came so rapidly that the children of Room 307 were unable to witness them. Ms. Sontag resorted instead to showing the class photographs of

*The cockroach, the cockroach, / Can't walk anymore, / Because it doesn't have, because it's lacking, / Its two little back feet.

caterpillars morphing. Now the chrysalises hung in a cage surrounded by netting, their silent presence foreshadowing change yet to come.

Room 307 was changing as well. Seating had been rearranged and groups of children reorganized. Six clusters of desks were turned into tables arranged in a circular fashion. At each table three children were busy following a recipe entitled "Insectos en Lodo," *Insects in Mud.*

In response to the first direction, "Abren 5 Oreos y quiten la crema con un cuchillo,"* Enrique eagerly began dismantling cookies and stuffing the sweet filling into his mouth. "The teacher said that's bad for you," Veronica reminded him. But her scolding ceased when Enrique agreed to share the white goo with her and Marisol.

The recipe called for "2 tazas de leche en un cuenco,"† so Marisol picked up a quarter-cup measure and prepared to pour the milk. A short time earlier, in a teacher-led discussion, the class had decided that four half-cups equal two cups, eight quarter-cups equal two cups, and two quarter-cups equal one half-cup. Marisol knew how much milk to pour, but she lacked the skill to get it all into the bowl. A white puddle soon collected on her desk.

When Ms. Sontag arrived to assist, Veronica held out a spoon and asked her teacher if they could use it, "¿Maestra, podemos usar ésto?" The teacher nodded her consent as she helped pour the milk, then left to help another group. Marisol poured chocolate pudding mix into the bowl of milk and began to stir.

"It looks like caca," Enrique observed.

"Marisol, you're doing all the work," Veronica protested. Enrique took over the stirring but Veronica was still dissatisfied. "Let's all take turns," she suggested, and the others nodded their agreement. Marisol and Enrique held the bowl down firmly as Veronica stirred. When they had finished, Enrique ran his finger around the rim of the bowl and then stuck it in his mouth.

"Don't eat it, you know, you might get sick," Veronica cautioned.

The recipe then directed: "Pongan las galletas en un plato y pongan otro plato encima de ellos. Aplasten las galletas."‡ Veronica picked up a

---

Open 5 Oreos and take the creme out with a spoon.
†*2 cups of milk in a bowl.*
‡*Put the cookies on a plate and put another plate on top of them. Flatten the cookies.*

cremeless Oreo and began to crumble it, creating a mess on the table below. "Here, you fix it up," she said to Enrique, who was happy to oblige, nibbling a few crumbs as he did so.

As they finished, Ms. Sontag began distributing gummy worms and raisins, which the children promptly divided according to the written instructions. Enrique and Marisol then spooned the chocolate pudding into three separate plastic cups. Veronica dipped her fingers into what chocolate remained in the bowl, licked her fingers, then cleaned them on her shorts. After sprinkling Oreo crumbs over the top of their pudding molds, the three cooks finished off their creation by pressing the candy and raisin bugs into the chocolate.

The ten-point recipe in Spanish had now been followed. "Insectos en Lodo" was ready to be set aside for an afternoon snack during Yo Leo, the daily period when their teacher read aloud.

"Maestra, dónde lo pongo?" Veronica inquired where to put the pudding cups, which she held on a freshly cleaned tray. Ms. Sontag told her to leave them on a counter near the back of the room.

"¡Maestra, puedes comerlo!" Veronica protested. *Teacher, you could eat them!* The class knew all about Ms. Sontag's sweet tooth.

"No te preocupes." *Don't you worry.*

Chocolate smeared across her own chin, Veronica looked skeptical but complied. Six trays, each containing three cups of pudding, now rested in front of the cage of brown cocoons.

Ms. Sontag was ready for the final morning announcement: "Hoy, en el almuerzo, ustedes pueden decirle a sus amigos que les hicieron insectos en lodo y que se los van a comer esta tarde." *Today at lunch you all can tell your friends that you made insects in mud and you are going to eat them this afternoon.*

A Recipe for Reading

In children's everyday world, distinctions between activities are not as rigid as they are in the traditional classroom. Students don't spontaneously practice reading skills to learn how to read; nor do they isolate reading as a singular activity. They read for a purpose, either for pleasure or to obtain information while engaged in other activities, like listening to music or eating breakfast. The same is true when it comes to acquiring language.

Ms. Sontag brings Spanish reading into an authentic context when she instructs the children to follow a recipe for a tasty snack —the results to be enjoyed later during Yo Leo. In other words, her teaching respects the natural way that children both learn to read and acquire language: by communicating in the context of purposeful activities and in concert with others.

New Birth

"They're worms! They're like earthworms!" Veronica exclaimed, as she finished her pudding left over from Yo Leo and inspected the small jar that Ms. Sontag had placed on the Resultados table. Thin, elongated bugs, about a centimeter in length, slithered up the sides to the lid, now equipped with tiny air holes. The rock-eggs had finally hatched.

When her teacher asked what the children thought the eggs had become, Veronica changed her mind and speculated that they were "arañitas." Leticia guessed "orugas," while Enrique proposed the idea of "un tipo de oruga."* When it became clear that none of the children knew the answer, Ms. Sontag jumped in.

"Estos son bebés. ¿Ustedes creen que son bebés como las ninfas o como la larva?" *They are babies. Is a baby like a nymph or a larva?*

"¡Larva!" the children responded, this time correctly.

"Larva," Ms. Sontag confirmed. "Son larvas. Son larvas de un insecto que se llama gusano de seda, gusano de seda." *They are larvae of an insect called a silkworm.*

She continued: "¿Saben qué es seda? ¿Alguien aquí sabe qué es seda? Ya, este material es bien, bien suave, bien ... muy bien, para la ropa. También es caro, es muy caro." *Do you know what seda means, this material that's very smooth, like certain clothing, and that's also very expensive?*

"Silk," Amber remarked, matter of factly, to no one in particular.

"My mom likes silk, but she doesn't like gusanos," Andy added.

With the newly hatched creatures identified, Ms. Sontag announced

Little spiders ... caterpillars ... a type of caterpillar.

that it was time to begin new calendars to keep track of them. "Vamos a empezar un calendario nuevo. Vamos a ver qué pasa con estos gusanitos." *We're going to see what happens with these baby worms.*

Veronica peered at the chocolate smeared all over her hands and asked whether she could go wash them. "¿Puedo lavar mis manos?"

"En un momentito," her teacher said. *In a little while.* "¿En qué mes estamos?" *What month is it?*

"Mayo, veintiuno," Marisol answered. *May 21.*

"Sí, mayo, aquí ponemos mayo. Ustedes van a llenarlo con los números." Ms. Sontag said. *Okay, May. So you are going to have to fill in the dates.* "¿En qué día empieza el uno?" *What day is the first?*

"Miércoles." Dylan volunteered. *Wednesday.*

"Miércoles, okay."

The girls and boys began to fill in their calendars, beginning with Wednesday. Veronica had a question. "Maestra, ¿cuántos días, treinta o treinta y uno?" she asked. *How many days, thirty or thirty-one?*

Ms. Sontag was involved with another group, so Naomi paged through a calendar on her lap until she discovered the number of days in May.

After the dates had been registered, Ms. Sontag directed the children's attention to the front of the room. Everyone wrote an "A" under May 14 and a "B" under May 21. At the bottom of the page, next to the letter A, they decided to write "Llegaron los huevos." *The eggs arrived.* Under B they chose "La larvas de los gusanos de seda salieron de los huevos." *The silkworm larvae left the eggs.*

Now it was time to set up a silkworm habitat. Ms. Sontag sat on the floor inside the ring of tables. Beside her was a cardboard box containing a few freshly picked green leaves. She called the children to the center of the room, one group at a time. Those who were not working with the silkworms wrote in their "diarios," *diaries.*

When it was her turn, Veronica gently stroked the silkworm larvae out of the jar and into the box with a paintbrush, her fingers placed on the handle, far from the bristles. The task proved harder than she had anticipated; the larvae clung to the plastic walls like glue. Her concentration was fierce, however, and Ms. Sontag assisted. Together with César, Naomi, and Enrique, they brushed the reluctant larvae into the home they now shared with the other developing silkworms. The children of Room 307 would watch for the next change.

Disequilibrium and Inquiry

According to constructivist theory, when we can make sense of our world, we are in a state of equilibrium. When this balance is upset, when things turn out differently from what we expect, we experience the opposite sensation. This state of *dis*equilibrium, prompting us to reconcile what we know (or think we know) with what we are now experiencing, creates ideal conditions for learning.

The struggle for understanding, however, must take place within a child's *zone of proximal development,* the distance between what students can do on their own and what they can accomplish with the help of a knowledgeable adult. In other words, the task should be within their intellectual grasp—not too difficult—or learning will be elusive. Nor should it be too easy, or children will not be challenged to construct new mental models of how the world works.

Social interaction can provide significant help in constructing meaning. So can *scaffolding,* temporary support offered by the teacher until students can proceed independently with a learning task. Veronica's equilibrium has been disturbed by the transformation of the rock-eggs. She changes her mind multiple times, but cannot figure out what the eggs have become. Ms. Sontag initiates a process that brings Veronica and her classmates back to a state of equilibrium. She provides scaffolds in the form of questioning, class discussion, and the process of scientific inquiry. Part of what the children are learning is that there will be more change to come.

The Toothless Cockroach

WRAPPED IN A GREEN AND WHITE TOWEL, hair glistening with droplets of water, Veronica bounced around her family's apartment, bubbling with energy. In her fingers she held a precious gem, a fallen tooth. She smiled repeatedly as she showed her mother, Leah, a gap just to the right of her two front teeth. Tonight the tooth fairy would be visiting.

"¡Mami, yo toqué un escarabajo!" she said. "¡Y yo toqué una mariposa, un poquitito parte de la mariposa!" *I touched a beetle and a butterfly, a tiny part of the butterfly!*

"¿De veras?" a skeptical Leah replied. *Really?*

"¡Mami, yo toqué un escarabajo muerto! Yo toqué un escarabajo viejo!" *I touched a dead beetle, an old beetle!*

"¿De veras?"

"Just kidding." Veronica switched languages for her English-dominant mom. She danced around the dining room table, singing the well-known song about the cockroach who could not walk due to a missing leg.

> *La cucaracha, la cucaracha,*
> *Ya no puede caminar,*
> *Porque no tiene, porque le falta,*
> *Las dos patitas de atrás.*

Veronica could have continued, but the thought of waking to a surprise from the tooth fairy provided strong motivation to go to bed. On arising the next morning, she entered her parents' bedroom, a dollar bill in her hand, singing an original verse about a cockroach who could not eat because of a missing tooth.

> *La cucaracha, la cucaracha,*
> *Ya no puede comer,*
> *Porque no tiene, porque le falta,*
> *El diente de atrás.**

At Home with Bugs

Veronica's thoughts about insects don't stop when she leaves Ms. Sontag's room. Because she is having fun at school, she is able to playfully integrate what she is learning at school into her family rituals. Her mother is happy to oblige. For this family, the second-grade curriculum at Inter-American is easy to connect to the real world because it is relevant and interesting.

**The cockroach, the cockroach, / Can't eat anymore, / Because it doesn't have, because it's lacking, / His back tooth.*

❦ CHAPTER SIX ❦

Beetles and Butterflies

*We were learning about discrimination and
social justice and racism—like real racism—not
racism that they teach you in a textbook but the
kind you experience every day. In a way, the city
was discriminating against Inter-American
because they were not giving us funding. We were
left in a school building that was supposed to be
temporary; it was there for twenty-five, thirty
years. ... We were the outcasts, the underdogs.
We weren't supposed to win, but we won!*

—Inter-American graduate
(Puerto Rican female)

TWO MIXED-GENDER LINES formed in the small hallway outside the classroom. Ms. Sontag, speaking in Spanish, told the children that another change had occurred. She also cautioned them not to express their enthusiasm as they had on Wednesday, an especially loud day.

Wendell peeked through the hallway and surveyed the room. "Look over there, look over there!" he shouted, but at least he didn't scream. Alicia spotted the butterflies next. "¡Mariposas!" she proclaimed.

As Ms. Sontag stepped aside, children flocked to the caterpillar habitat. Five empty chrysalises, cracked and dry like mealworm skins, hung from the top of the cage. Four butterflies clung motionless to the net, while one rested on red paper petals below. Their wings were a mix of black flecked with white and orange flecked with black, although only one displayed its colors with open wings.

Excited gasps followed: "Ooooooooohhhhh! ... Watch, watch ... They think that paper is a flower! ... Mueva, Joaquin! ... Look at this one, Camilo, lookit, lookit! ... Teacher, what about these colors? ... Come here. ... Two, three! ... Oh! Four, five! ... Lookit, lookit, he's trying to fly!"

Veronica and Amber remained near the front hallway, deep in conversation. After a few minutes they, too, joined the children clustered in front of the butterflies.

César gently parted the crowd. Enrique put his right arm over Veronica's shoulder and drew her in closer to the net. Dylan walked over and teased the group, telling them, in grammatically flawed Spanish, to go to their tables: "¡Va a tu mesas!"

Veronica examined the butterflies and then walked toward her table. Damion, seated in his chair, tried to catch her attention. "I have a flipper toy," he said, looking up at her longingly.

"Sooooooooo?" Veronica replied coolly, and walked away, avoiding a conversation.

Ms. Sontag signaled the end of the observation period by turning off the lights. The flutter of children and butterflies died down as the boys and girls returned to their tables.

"Mesa seis es la más callada," she said, singling out Table 6 as the quietest. The class giggled. Amber was not in her seat, and Liset and Beatríz had not yet arrived at school. Nobody else was assigned to Table 6.

Ms. Sontag cautioned that the butterflies were easily frightened and that the children needed to speak softly when they were near the cage. Then came a most welcome announcement; they would spend the rest of the morning practicing for the Pan American Assembly.

Veronica put on her white Caribbean-style costume, a ruffled blouse and matching skirt. As a cassette tape beat African drums, she was transformed, her full skirt whirling like a butterfly's wings, by the rhythm of the Puerto Rican Bomba.

Counteracting the Prevalence of English

The separation of language for instructional purposes, a guiding principle of dual immersion, helps to develop competence in both languages. A lesson should be conducted in English or Spanish, but not in both. Otherwise students tend to ignore input in their weaker language. In effective immersion programs, both one-way and two-way, teachers make certain that their students understand the linguistic parameters of the classroom.

In Room 307, the dominant influence of English is quite obvious. While these curious and energetic second-graders are easily drawn into the realm of bugs and butterflies, encouraging them to speak in Spanish is more complicated. Ms. Sontag uses her professional judgment to make choices on when and how to reinforce second-language acquisition. She does nothing to prohibit children's interactions in English, so as to avoid dampening their enthusiasm about the butterflies. Instead, she patiently persists in using Spanish during science study, even when students revert to English. In order to share their fascinating discoveries, as well as to enjoy their teacher's humor, the children must interact with the class in Spanish. Even during the free-flowing butterfly observation, Dylan's humorous directive in Spanish reflects the power of teacher modeling.

Love and Marriage

CHANGE CAN BE DISTURBING AND PAINFUL. On Monday afternoon a butterfly died. Previously the class had been nonchalant about the passing of several beetles, but a butterfly was a different matter. Downcast, the children theorized about what had happened. Though no one could be certain, the most accepted explanation was that, in its struggle to free itself from the chrysalis, the butterfly had taken a fall, resulting in a mortal injury.

Liset worried that the other butterflies might come to harm. But Leticia noted that they were already out of their chrysalises. If the class took good care of them, she argued, they should be fine.

In fact, the four remaining butterflies were thriving, and Ms. Sontag reminded the group that they needed tending. The students were still engaged in the process of scientific study and thus continued their observations. They learned how butterflies "chupan su comida," *suck their food,* through a "probóscide," *proboscis,* or "nariz especial," *special nose.* Their teacher guided them in predicting what future changes might occur.

Naomi speculated, "Van a ponerse más grandes." *They're going to get bigger.*

"Y volar más," suggested Marisol. *And fly more.*

"Vamos a mirar más huevos," Ms. Sontag predicted. *We're going to see more eggs.* The children liked this idea very much and embellished upon the theme: "¡Van a tener bebés! They're going to have babies. ... They're gonna get married!"

Unfortunately, these butterflies, the classroom's beloved "Damas Pintadas," *Painted Ladies,* had just two more weeks to live. It was also two weeks until the close of the school year. Would the children of Room 307 experience the final phase in the life cycle of a butterfly?

Conceptual Learning

Ms. Sontag avoids drilling students on isolated facts about insects. Instead, she stresses concepts in the context of hands-on activity and observation. The overarching theme of the insect curriculum is change as it applies to the life cycle of living organisms. Eventually the children should be able to apply their understanding beyond the classroom in broader life contexts apart from insects.

Ms. Sontag is aware that this reflective transfer of knowledge will occur over time. Its full impact cannot be measured in a single school year, nor with the multiple-choice tests administered every spring. But there are aspects of learning that she can see—and facilitate immediately—and this is where she concentrates her efforts. By introducing a scientific approach to observing change and collecting data, she guides the children in making predictions about future change. Her focus on conceptual learning promotes the development of critical thinking.

Green Hand Syndrome

"Maestra, ¡ya sé como hacerlo!" Veronica boasted. *I already know how to do it!*

Before Ms. Sontag could finish her demonstration to the class, the child took a sheet of tissue paper and began forming the petals of a flower. "Maestra, ¿puedo hacer ésto?" *Could she continue?* Ms. Sontag smiled.

"Así,"* Veronica sighed with satisfaction as she pulled another petal into position. When every tissue was in its place, she called her teacher over to look. "¡Mira, maestra!"

Veronica surveyed her work once again. Fluffing out the red, white, and peach petals, she formed a hollow space in the center of the flower and inserted a wad of black tissue, creating what looked like a multicolored black-eyed susan.

The project of the afternoon was to create an artistic representation of each phase of development in the life cycle of a butterfly: huevo, oruga (o larva), crisálida, y mariposa.† Each of these creatures would then be attached to the flower, with the egg nestled in its petals and the chrysalis hanging from it.

Soon the artwork began to take shape, emerging from a combination of clay, tissue and construction paper, paint, pipe cleaners, and egg cartons. Of particular fascination to the children was the tempera paint used to color the caterpillars. When Ms. Sontag asked the class what they thought the green and yellow paint was for, Naomi correctly responded that it was to make stripes: "Para hacer rayas." As the paintbrushes were distributed, Veronica held one up and asked whether she and her classmates could begin: "Maestra, ¿podemos empezar?"

After Ms. Sontag nodded her consent, Dylan used his paintbrush to cover his egg carton with a green base. Across the room, however, Amber had a different idea. She announced in English that she preferred to use her fingers. This idea received a less than positive response from Ms. Sontag. But Dylan joined in, abandoning his brush to rub green paint into cardboard crevices, first with his fingers and then with his

---

Like this.
†*Egg, caterpillar (or larva), chrysalis, and butterfly.*

entire palm. The underside of his hand soon turned the deep green color of the paint.

The green hand syndrome began to spread like a contagious disease. At a nearby table, both sides of Beatríz's hands were coated in dark green from her wrist to the tips of her fingers. Camilo, Andy, Damion, and Manny had also followed Amber's example; now their hands were in various stages of coloration. Manny reached out to Dylan and placed a green hand on the front of his shirt. Dylan grinned and reciprocated by giving his friend a green handprint on the back of his.

But not everything was a shade of green. "¡Maestra, mira qué pasó!" *Look what happened!* Veronica cried out, pointing to the yellow paint spilled on her desk. She went to the saloncito to get cleanup supplies and began to scrub her desktop as the classroom cassette player churned out the words to "Las Hormiguitas," a song about little ants.

Ms. Sontag was not pleased. She sent all of the wayward artists to assist in the cleanup.

"Teacher, can I wash my hands first?" Amber, who had started it all, apparently had had enough.

"¿Cómo?"

Amber took the hint and restated her request in Spanish. "¿Puedo lavar mis manos?" She ended up in the bathroom trying to figure out how she had managed to get green spots on the back of her shirt.

"Las Hormiguitas" finished playing and was replaced by a children's version of the "Jarabe Tapatío."

"Maestra, that's the music from our dance class!" Marisol announced, as she and Naomi began to tap out the steps they had learned to the Mexican Hat Dance.

It was important to clean up quickly. Today was Wendell's birthday and a small celebration awaited. Her projects now complete, Veronica rocked her cardboard caterpillar back and forth, squeaking out a high pitched "qui qui, qui qui, qui qui." Then she started singing "Las Mañanitas," the traditional Mexican birthday song:

Estas son las mañanitas
Que cantaba el Rey David
A las muchachas bonitas,
Te las cantamos así.

Despierta, mi bien, despierta,
Mira lo que almaneció,
Ya los pajaritos cantan,
La luna ya se metió. *

The Power of Art

Ms. Sontag understands the motivational power of arts-based activities in fostering academic knowledge as well as second-language acquisition. In this instance, she uses visual art to reinforce science vocabulary. Meanwhile, in the background, she plays children's music in Spanish to create a pleasant ambiance. An additional benefit is that, because music is subconsciously linked to memory, it can enhance second-language development.

The teacher's efforts seem to be having an effect. When English-dominant Veronica finishes creating her caterpillar, she gives it a voice using Spanish phonology. This is an indication that Veronica is beginning to internalize Spanish.

The Great Bug Escape

THE BUTTERFLIES HAD ESCAPED AGAIN. The beetles, too, continued their quest for freedom. Even some of the now-orange-and-black insectos de algodoncillo, the milkweed bugs, had managed to sneak out. Ms. Sontag caught one of these, and the class watched as it unfolded its probóscide while resting on her hand.

The Great Bug Escape repeated itself almost every morning. The first time, about twenty beetles were discovered under a book. As Ms. Sontag lifted it up, the insects scurried away until Alicia and Damion helped return them to their specially constructed habitat. When a butterfly escaped, Alicia caught it with a fishnet and put it back in the cage.

The next day, in the middle of math class, Amber exclaimed, "There's an insecto de algodoncillo crawling up the string!" Her teacher thought it was just a cockroach, but Amber was adamant, insisting that it was a milkweed bug.

*This is the morning song / That King David sang / To the pretty girls, / As we sing it to you. / Wake up, my love, wake up, / Look at what dawn has brought, / Already the little birds are singing, / The moon has set.

Two more escaped butterflies were soon spotted; one was caught in a vent. Ms. Sontag helped it crawl onto her finger, and the children watched intently as she placed it back in the butterfly cage. The other butterfly was caught by Enrique wielding a fishnet and was put back as well.

Still, the children were not satisfied. Despite Ms. Sontag's claim that it was a cockroach, they insisted there was an *insecto de algodoncillo* climbing on a string hanging from a poster on the wall. Finally, she relented, climbed on top of a desk, and was relieved to discover that the children were correct. But another bug was soon spotted crawling on the floor. *Insectos de algodoncillo* were escaping all over the place!

Liset was concerned. "Why do you think they keep trying to escape?" she asked Andy.

"Well," he said, "they probably smell the food from the cafeteria and once they smell it they start trying to come out. I found some dead ones right near my seat, and I got to bring them home to look at."

"Yuck!" grunted Liset, as her upper lip curled toward her nose.

"Oh, the dead ones are not bad," Andy explained, enjoying his bug-expert status. "It's the live ones that are yucky. The first time that you get at least seven or eight or nine beetles on your finger, they start chopping you up, or they start poking at you, and they try to smell your hand."

Ms. Sontag gently removed the *insecto de algodoncillo* from the string. When she stepped down from the desk, the children clustered around and spontaneous insect observation ensued. Of special interest was the *probóscide* that sucks food, nutrients, and liquids. They noted that it was like the butterfly's as opposed to the beetle's. The class continued to make observations as the insect crawled around on their teacher's hand before being imprisoned once again in its cage.

Teachable Moments

Ms. Sontag creates an environment conducive to extemporaneous learning experiences, also known as *teachable moments.* Such opportunities are routinely present in most classrooms, yet pressure to cover the required subject matter often keeps teachers from exploiting them. When the process of learning is natural and unhurried, neither a "race" nor another form of competition, fascinating detours can be explored rather than avoided. In this case, Ms. Sontag uses the Great Bug Escape to encourage both scientific observation and the use of Spanish in the classroom.

This teachable moment is possible because she has based her science teaching on a topic of inherent interest to the children. Not only are they are fascinated by insects; they are also able to observe them in their out-of-school lives. The learning experiences in this science unit are thus authentic rather than contrived.

Beetles

NAOMI AND MARISOL STARED DOWN at the riot of black beetles tunneling through a carpet of oatmeal. Rotting pieces of apple were scattered throughout the rectangular bin, and the hungry insects swarmed over them like locusts on a feeding binge. The two girls, faces frozen in disgust, contemplated their unsavory mission: Feed the beetles to get their minds off escape.

The fat, crawling bugs needed a fresh supply of fruit. But first, the remainders of last week's meals had to be removed. Neither child volunteered to begin. Marisol picked up a napkin lying on the table and handed it to Naomi. "Use this," she advised.

Naomi wrinkled her nose. "It might crawl on the napkin." Marisol was silent. Covering her hand, Naomi used the napkin to grab a chunk of rotting apple, but it slipped from her fingers. "It's too slimy," she said.

Marisol still said nothing, as Naomi tried again, this time with more success. She scooped up the decayed fruit quickly and then dropped it on the table as if it were poison. She repeated the procedure with several other pieces.

"Now you get one. I've done all of them," she said, handing the napkin to Marisol, who distastefully declined. Only one piece of apple was left, and it seemed that all of the displaced beetles had flocked to it. The children stood motionless above the beetle habitat.

"It's got escarabajos on it," Marisol muttered. The two continued to stare. "Maybe if we, like, put a new apple in, they'll go to the new one and we can, like, get the old one."

Naomi agreed to the plan. She began cutting a chunk from a leftover apple, but the warm, dark pulp resisted the knife. Finally giving up, the girls went to speak to Ms. Sontag, with Naomi as spokesperson. "Maestra, it's all ... toda la manzana es vieja y soft." *The apple is old and soft.* "¿Tienes otro?" *Do you have another one?* she asked.

Ms. Sontag sent them off to the cafeteria and they returned with a fresh apple. Naomi sliced off a crisp chunk. "You can't cut it that big," Marisol protested. "Yes, I can," Naomi said. "Look at these." She pointed to the rotted chunks lying on the table. "They ate all of them."

The girls rotated the task of slicing, dropping the newly cut apples into the beetle habitat. As the insects swarmed to attack the fresh fruit, Marisol quickly plucked out the final rotten piece. Mission accomplished. The beetles could now be safely left for the weekend and Ms. Sontag was pleased.

Naomi asked, "What do beetles turn into?"

"We'll find out," her teacher answered.

Language and Friendships

By bringing together children of different linguistic backgrounds, dual immersion programs make friendships possible such as the one between Spanish-dominant Marisol and English-dominant Naomi. Ms. Sontag is aware of the special relationship that exists between these two girls. So she has placed them in situations that help them grow cognitively—in this case, by figuring out how to accomplish a distasteful task—while enjoying each other's company.

Ms. Sontag was also hoping that Naomi would benefit from an opportunity to converse with Marisol in Spanish. But even though Spanish is Marisol's first language and Naomi's Spanish proficiency is at a conversational level, the two friends choose to communicate almost exclusively in English. When they need to consult with their teacher, the interactions switch to Spanish, the designated language of insect study. Then they resume private conversation in English, the higher-status language. Nevertheless, Ms. Sontag's classroom policy fosters Naomi's Spanish-language development, and it also reminds Marisol that Spanish has value and prestige.

Although Marisol often speaks English in social situations, she still benefits from academic and reading instruction in her native language. Literacy in Spanish will further serve as a bridge to literacy development in English. For children like Marisol, who sense the dominant influence of the majority language, the desire to speak it well with classmates like Naomi helps to ensure they will achieve conversational competence in English. That, in turn, helps to promote academic competence in English. Less frequently noted, but of great importance, are the benefits to her self-esteem and identity construction.

Naomi in the Bug Garden

THE SALONCITO WAS NOW IN USE, transformed into the editorial office of *The Daily Bug Garden,* the official newspaper of Room 307. Naomi sat at the computer, looking tentatively at the keyboard and gingerly pressing keys. A capital *T* appeared in the upper left corner, followed by *o, d, a, y.* With meticulous precision, she began: "Today in class 307 they got new butterflies some have not come out of there cocoons and they are white." Then she paused, deep in thought.

Manny leaned in the doorway, fidgeting with impatience. He was the next journalist in line to use the computer and he knew that time was running out. The week was nearly over, and so was the school year.

When Ms. Sontag arrived, Naomi got back to work and added several more sentences. "All finished," the writer announced triumphantly. But her teacher noted that the story consisted of one long paragraph, and suggested the need for some editing. So Naomi made a few changes until she felt her report was ready to go to press:

> Today in class 307 they got new butterflies some have not come out of there cocoons and they are white.
>
> Everybody is excited. Leticia a second-grader felt that at first the butterflies were caterpillars then they were cocoons then they were butterflies but one died.
>
> Wendell and Damion said, "They first came out of the cocoon and one died. They put out garbage. It looked like blood."

Leticia also said that the butterflies' color was red, orange, black, and white. Liset said that the color of the butterflies' are orange white and black.

César said that he only knew that the butterflies came in May. Camilo said that they came to the class on Friday, May 27, 1996.

Cultivating Biliteracy

Both dual immersion and constructivist pedagogy encourage an *emergent literacy* perspective. In other words, literacy is developed in the course of meaningful and functional activities, such as the production of a class newspaper. Naomi is not being asked to complete a decontextualized exercise, but rather to write something for her classmates about an exciting classroom event. She has strong motivation to produce the news story because it has personal meaning for her.

While the assignment is in English, it also supports the goal of bilingualism because reading ability, like factual knowledge about insects, is transferable. As Stephen Krashen explains, "Once you can read, you can read"—in whatever language you go on to acquire.

In addition, the curriculum in English is thematically related to the curriculum in Spanish. Not only does this approach strengthen academic learning; the natural context also helps students to acquire vocabulary in both languages, without resorting to direct translation or memorization.

Butterflies

WENDELL AND ANDY ran frantically to Ms. Sontag. "Maestra!" Andy cried. "We think a mariposa is dying! It's on the floor on its side, and it's flapping its wings, and its probóscide is hanging down!"

Their teacher remained calm. She advised that the butterfly be left in peace while they finished their assignment: "Ahora tenemos que dejarle en paz. Seguimos con el trabajo y la chequeamos más tarde." *We'll go on with our work and check on it later.*

Just three days were left in the school year and many tasks had to be completed. Throughout the room children were involved in various end-of-year activities: putting together portfolios, cleaning out desks and backpacks, and writing letters to their as-yet-unknown third-grade teachers. The two boys rejoined the classroom flurry.

Forty minutes later Andy, still accompanied by Wendell, was back reporting to Ms. Sontag. "Look, it's shaking," he said, pointing toward the cage at the side of the room. "It's really sick. What's wrong?"

"¿Qué crees que está pasando?" their teacher responded. *What do you think is happening?* She made a point of switching to Spanish, the designated language of insect discovery. "¿Cómo sabes que está enfermo? ¿Podría ser otra cosa? ¿Qué lo hace temblar tanto?" *How do you know he's sick? Or could it be something else that's making it shake so hard?*

Ms. Sontag, followed by Andy and Wendell, walked over to the cage and visually examined the butterfly. "Mira en la flor. ¿Qué ven ustedes?" *Look at the flower. What do you see?*

"I dunno," Andy replied.

Ms. Sontag persisted. "Las cositas negras." *The little black things.*

"Oh yeah!"

"¿Qué son?" she asked what they were.

Wendell looked up at Ms. Sontag wide-eyed. Andy seemed unable to comprehend why his teacher would ask a question with such an obvious answer.

"¡Huevos!" they both declared, each with his own distinct intonation.

Eagerly they called over Leticia, José Luis, and Camilo, who were working nearby, while Ms. Sontag calmly beckoned to the others. In an instant children were clustered around the butterfly cage, some standing in front of it, others gazing down from the radiators, still others perched on chairs behind. All eyes were focused on a butterfly with its abdomen angled downward on the red paper flower. It was laying an egg.

Cautioned to be quiet by their teacher, the children reacted in excited whispers. "¡Están poniendo huevos! ... Come here, come here! ... ¿Maestra, qué hacen? ... Where are the huevos? ... Look, look, look! ... Oh look, I see one! ... ¡No toques!* ... I don't see them. ... On the flower! ... Maestra, maestra, the eggs are under the net! They fell down!"

The butterfly that had been reported as dying earlier was now laying its eggs on the net that rested just above the floor of the cage. Some of

They're laying eggs! ... Teacher, what are they doing? ... Don't touch!

the eggs already lay trapped between the netting and the hard plastic. Leticia's small hand reached inside to rescue them.

"No podemos tocarlos," cautioned Ms. Sontag. *We can't touch them.*

Wendell was wide-eyed once again. "So you're telling me that we're gonna have orugas crawling around under the net?" he asked.

Ms. Sontag had no answer but sent Leticia and Alicia to the saloncito to summon Naomi, Marisol, and Manny, who were at the computer working on *The Daily Bug Garden.* "The butterflies are laying eggs! The butterflies are laying eggs!" they proclaimed.

The three latecomers charged out of the storage room and maneuvered their way into the cluster of children standing in front of the butterfly cage. All were entranced by the tiny brown specks, smaller than a pinhead, and were breathlessly hoping for more. But the three students were too late; no new eggs emerged.

Children slowly trickled back to their seats. "Okay niños, ya es la hora para pasar a la presentación," Ms. Sontag announced. It was time to visit the sixth-grade inventors fair.

A few minutes later the children were walking down the hallway and Room 307 was empty. Almost. In a darkened corner, beetles scurried over spoiling chunks of apple. Milkweed bugs hanging in plastic bags sucked nourishment out of wet paper towels. Butterflies fluttered their wings, while minute brown eggs rested on paper petals, hiding within them unborn caterpillars.

Huevo, oruga, crisálida, mariposa, huevo. *Egg, caterpillar, chrysalis, butterfly, egg.* Change is continual. Life goes on.

Habits of Mind

Ms. Sontag sets up learning situations that require inference and prediction. Because she takes no immediate action in response to the children's concern about the butterfly's strange behavior, they are encouraged to speculate about what will happen next. In this case, remaining silent amid the drama is more useful than providing an immediate explanation. She understands that giving children some leeway to solve mysteries on their own will serve to stimulate their imaginations. Later she asks questions designed to promote critical thinking.

Opportunities for cognitive development were foremost in Ms. Sontag's mind when she developed this science unit. Thus she focuses as much on the process as on the content of learning. The subject matter provides a context in which children can develop critical habits of mind—for example, remembering to question how they know what they know.

Also noteworthy is that, for many of the students, the process occurs in a language they are still acquiring. One of the ideas behind immersion programs is that second-language acquisition occurs best when students are focused not on grammatical forms—nor, indeed, on language at all—but on natural activities such as problem-solving.

Alicia's Secret

ON FRIDAY MORNING MS. SONTAG arrived early. Much remained to be done to get ready for next week and the ending of school. As usual, Alicia was the first student to arrive, greeting her teacher warmly. "¡Buenos días, Maestra!"

Immediately they checked on the butterflies, which seemed quiet. Reassured that the insects needed no attention, Ms. Sontag left Alicia in the classroom while she went on an errand. On her return, she was greeted by an excited cry. "¡Maestra, hay una oruguita en la flor!" *There's a little caterpillar on the flower.*

Sure enough, there was a tiny caterpillar among the butterflies. Alicia couldn't wait to tell her friends, none of whom had yet arrived. Ms. Sontag put her finger to her lips. "Vamos a guardarlo como un secreto hasta que todos estén aquí," she said. *Let's keep this a secret until everyone gets here.* "Después puedes compartir tu descubrimiento con todos los niños y podemos hablar de lo que significa." *Then you can share your discovery with all the children and we can discuss what it means.*

Alicia was delighted by this plan. An hour later she was standing in front of her classmates. Ms. Sontag set the stage, encouraging her to describe her early-morning discovery: "Yo, esta mañana, miré a las mariposas y no vi nada. Entonces me fui abajo para hacer copias y cuando subí Alicia estaba en el salón. ¿Qué dijiste, Alicia?"*

Under the spotlight, the quiet girl became even shyer. But pride in her achievement soon prevailed, and she began to report on the morning's events. "Vi una oruga," she said. *I saw a caterpillar.*

"¿Una qué?" Ms. Sontag prompted. *A what?*

"Oruguita." *Little caterpillar.*

"¿Dónde?" *Where?*

"En la flor." *On the flower.*

"¿Pero tuvimos oruguitas ayer?" *But did we have little caterpillars yesterday?*

"No."

"No. ¿De dónde vino?" *So where did it come from?*

"Porque ayer una mariposa puso huevos y ahora tenemos una oruguita," Alicia explained. *Because yesterday a butterfly laid eggs and now we have a little caterpillar.*

The bare facts having been established, Ms. Sontag began to ask more probing questions to help the children determine exactly what these new creatures were. "La oruguita es, ¡qué cosa! ¿Es cómo qué? ¿Es un adulto? ¿Qué es? ... Una larva. Es una larva. ¿O? ... O un bebé. Voy a llamarles en grupitos de dos."†

After reviewing with her students that the caterpillar was a larva, she assigned Alicia to look for it. "Alicia va a buscar la oruga." The other children would be called, in pairs, to the butterfly cage to see the new arrival for themselves. She reminded them to speak in Spanish. "Niños, hablen español, por favor."

Spanish-dominant Alicia stood expectantly by the butterfly cage. Naomi and Marisol were the first partners sent to view the tiny caterpillar, which resembled a black piece of lint.

"Aaaaaaaahhhhhhhh!" Naomi's mouth hung open as she gazed downward in silence at the spot on the red paper petal.

This morning I looked at the butterflies and I didn't see anything. Then I went downstairs to make copies and when I came back up, Alicia was in the classroom. What did you say, Alicia?

†*The little caterpillar is—how strange!—is like what? Is it an adult? What is it? ... A larva. It's a larva. Or? ... Or a baby. I'm going to call you in pairs.*

Finally, words came to her. "Now it looks like a huevo."

"En español," Alicia whispered.

"Un huevo chiquito," Naomi said. *A tiny egg.*

"No, más pequeño," Marisol countered. *Smaller.* She pinched her thumb and her third finger together to illustrate.

Not to be outdone, Naomi brought her fingers even closer. "No, es como está puntito," she argued. *It's like this little dot.*

"Es como ... así." *Like this.* Marisol made her imaginary egg tinier still.

Diplomatically, Alicia nodded her agreement with both girls. "Está bien chiquitito," she said. *It's really small.*

Two by two, the other children were sent to be hosted by Alicia as they observed the oruguita. Dylan fantasized about what could happen next. "What if that egg breaks open and a huge caterpillar comes out? What if a butterfly comes out of the egg? So where is he? Where is he? How many eggs are there?"

Alicia replied patiently to each of her classmates. "¿La ves? ¿La cosa negra? Salió de ese huevo. Do you see that black thing by the leaf? See it move? Y salió de ese huevo. Okay, Ms. Sontag, ya terminé la mesa seis." She continued with the next group. "Salió de ese huevo aquí. Mira."*

"How do you know it's an oruguita?" Beatríz asked.

"Because salió de ese huevo y se mueve mucho." *Because it came out of this egg and it moves a lot.* Gently, like her teacher, Alicia reminded each small group to communicate in Spanish.

After everyone had had a turn to view the caterpillar, Veronica returned for a second look. To her dismay, it was no longer visible. "Maybe it fell down in the water," she said sadly.

While she searched for the caterpillar, Amber, Dylan, Camilo, and Leticia were watching the beetles. Amber observed a new insect activity. "They're mating!" She called out excitedly, catching Ms. Sontag's attention. "Teacher, are they mating?"

"¿Cómo lo vamos a saber?" Ms. Sontag responded again with questions. *How are we going to know?* "En una semana, más o menos, ¿qué va a pasar?" *In a week or so, what's going to happen?*

"They'll have babies," Amber replied.

Do you see it? The black thing? It came out of this egg. ... Okay, Ms. Sontag, Table 6 has finished. ... It came out of this egg here. Look.

"¿Qué son los bebés?" *What kind of babies?*

Simultaneously, the children answered "gusanos" or "larva."

Amber was still looking down at the beetle habitat, fascinated. "They're mating!"

"What's that mean?" Camilo was perplexed.

"You don't know what mating is?" Dylan asked in amazement.

Amber supplied the answer: "Having sex."

"Go away! Give them privacy!" scolded Leticia.

Overhearing these tantalizing tidbits of conversation, Andy and Liset rushed over. Watching beetles having sex had more appeal than searching for a lost caterpillar. "C'mon Liset, leave them alone. Give them some privacy," Leticia persisted, trying to shoo her away. But Andy got the final word. "They're fighting over a woman," he announced.

Gradually insect-watching turned into room cleanup. Eggs might be hatching, but the school year was still drawing to a conclusion. Everyone had jobs to do.

Naomi sorted books with Marisol in the library corner. One at a time they placed the Spanish volumes in a blue plastic bin and the English volumes in a white one. Beatríz lay on her side, her head resting on the sofa cushion, reading a book. The other girls did not seem to mind that she was not helping. Wendell, Damion, and Dylan used yardsticks to push magnets from high off the wall. Manny scrubbed desktops with soap and water.

Liset started to gather up her things. "There's bugs under my cubby!" she squealed. But it was a false alarm. "What's this?" She pulled out a set of worn red earmuffs.

All around the room, posters and papers were coming down. "Will other kids be coming here?" Beatríz asked tentatively, as if sensing a betrayal.

"Yes, there will be new children in the room next fall," Ms. Sontag said tenderly, as if new caterpillars were about to be born, or milkweed bug larvae were going to emerge from silent eggs.

"Oh," Beatríz responded, without a smile.

"Magic carpet, magic carpet," announced Amber joyfully, as she headed toward Table 6 carrying a large yellow paper over her head.

Ms. Sontag stood in the middle of the fray counting lunch money and preparing meal tickets. There was no time to joke about chocolate-covered beetles today. Yet she paused amid the swirling voices, a wave of melancholy washing through her. She would miss them all.

Andy, the muralist. Naomi, the budding journalist. Amber, who should have been named Green. Dylan, waiting for a butterfly to pop out of a tiny egg. Enrique, with his uncontrollable craving for Oreos. Marisol, who had had a mealworm named in her honor. Manny, who wished his mealworm was really a lightning bug. Damion and his flipper toy. Leticia, determined to protect the privacy of beetles. Alicia, who had been enchanted to discover the newborn caterpillar. Veronica, the drama queen. And Beatríz, who was so sad the school year was ending.

Students as Teachers

In traditional models of education, there are sharp distinctions between the roles of teachers and students. Not so in constructivist classrooms. Teachers learn alongside their students, and students become teachers or sometimes facilitators of the learning environment. Ms. Sontag takes advantage of Alicia's discovery, giving her a chance to facilitate her peers' learning of both subject matter and language.

In addition, by discussing an exciting new development with Alicia in front of the other children, Ms. Sontag seizes opportunities to model conversation in Spanish with a native speaker, both to promote respect for the minority language in the classroom and to reinforce positive self-esteem in Alicia. A bilingual peer group provides a rich resource for second-language development, and Ms. Sontag uses it wisely.

CHAPTER SEVEN

Goodbye, Mrs. Bee

*I see students from other schools and they
might be smart, but they are kind of like
robots. Schools like that, whatever they teach,
they just make kids spit it back out on paper.
I think Inter-American let us be ourselves.*

—Inter-American graduate
(Mexican/African-American female)

TWELVE CHILDREN SHOWED UP for class on Monday, the final full
day of school. Andy and Enrique were already vacationing with
their families. Amber was ill and had phoned in her request for a place
in the butterfly lottery. Nobody had heard from Liset, Joaquin, or Damion. Wherever they were, they missed out on a nonstop bug party led
by the tireless Ms. Sontag.

Games and crafts went on all morning. First, the children created
their own probóscides to use in the lunchroom, where they would show
off their bug knowledge to the entire school. Dramatizations followed,
first individually and then in pairs, as the class acted out the "etapas,"
stages, in the lives of a gusano de harina, an escarabajo, and a mariposa.

Finally came a competition to see who could correctly mime insect
motions in ten seconds, before Ms. Sontag could count them "out." The
words *huevo, oruga, crisálida,* and *mariposa* were suddenly flying out of
her mouth. Counting so fast that the numbers became a blur, she moved

like a frantic beetle trying to escape her vial. The children shrieked with delight. One by one, consumed with giggles, they were banished to the floor. After calm was partially restored, they picked up their probóscides and headed for the cafeteria in dramatic style.

In the afternoon the pace of activity intensified, as Ms. Sontag led them in a Spanish-language version of "hangman"; the secret word was A̲ B̲ E̲ J̲ A̲ S̲. When the game ended, she left the main room, announcing "Tengo que encontrar una invitada especial." *I have to meet a special guest.* Soon after, someone stepped out of the saloncito wearing the attire of a beekeeper and carrying a large wooden box with lots of interesting supplies.

"Yo me llamo Señora Abe Ja y yo trabajo con abejas," she said. *My name is Mrs. Abe Ja and I work with bees.* Yo, en mi trabajo, yo soy una colmenera. ¿Ustedes saben qué es una colmena?" *I am a beekeeper. Do you know what a beehive is?*

"You're Ms. Sontag!" César shouted.

"¿Quién es Ms. Sontag? ¿Es una abeja?" Señora Abe Ja asked. *Who is Ms. Sontag? Is she a bee?*

The mysterious guest went on to describe her work, including the intricacies of life in a beehive and the work of a beekeeper. Because the children had studied the life cycle of other insects, Señora Abe Ja included a discussion of the life cycle of a bee. While some children asked questions about bees, others focused elsewhere.

Dylan's hand waved rapidly in the air as he chanted "¡Abe, Abe, Abe Ja! ¡Abe, Abe, Abe Ja! ¡Abe, Abe, Abe Ja!"

"Is this the stuff your father does or something?" inquired Wendell.

Señora Abe Ja could not respond to the question because she did not understand English. But she did share a tremendous amount of information about bees and beehives, and she had authentic attire and equipment as well.

"¡Abe, Abe, Abe Ja! ¡Abe, Abe, Abe Ja! ¡Abe, Abe, Abe Ja!" The noise level continued to rise. Señora Abe Ja became silent. Dylan, the instigator of the chanting, scolded his classmates. "Stop talking. She's waiting. Whatever her name is."

"Abeja," several classmates responded. "¡Abe, Abe!" The wild chatter resumed.

"She's waiting, now stop talking!" Dylan persisted. "Ssshhh!" Relative quiet returned, and for a time the children continued with serious questioning in Spanish.

"Tengo una pregunta," Dylan said, staring intently at the strange visitor. *I have a question.* Señora Abe Ja nodded in his direction. "¿Tú sabes mucho de las abejas?" *Do you know a lot about bees?*

"Sí, es mi trabajo," she replied. *Yes, it's my work.*

"Mi maestra también sabe mucho de las abejas," Dylan replied. *My teacher also knows a lot about bees.*

Señora Abe Ja then called on Marisol. "¿Por qué las flores tienen néctar?" the girl asked.

"¡Buena pregunta!" Mrs. Bee exclaimed. *Great question!* Then she began a detailed response about why flowers have nectar.

Meanwhile, Dylan had not finished. "Señora Abeja, mi maestra tiene la misma ropa que tú tienes," he said. *My teacher has the same clothes that you have.*

"¡Y tambien la misma cara que tú tienes!" *Also the same face that you have!* César added, to general hilarity.

As Mrs. Bee answered the children's final questions, Dylan, Manny, Beatríz, and Naomi crept silently into the saloncito and hid behind doors or under tables. They were determined to watch the familiar-looking beekeeper transform herself into Ms. Sontag (who was unable to shoo them away). Yet, despite the overwhelming evidence, Ms. Sontag never acknowledged who had been playing the role of Señora Abe Ja. Exiting the saloncito, she returned to her students, expressed regret at missing the special visitor, and immediately began the next activity.

On small slips of paper, each child wrote down the name of his or her favorite bug, then folded it for secrecy. Rhythm instruments were distributed, and students were instructed to practice making a sound that would convey the essence of their chosen insect. A guessing game ensued. Beetles and butterflies were heavily represented, but a few other creatures, such as grasshoppers and lightning bugs, slipped in as well.

After each child had had a turn at the front of the room, Ms. Sontag took center stage. She played a recording of Rimsky-Korsakov's "Flight of the Bumblebee" and asked the children what insect it reminded them of. They all guessed quickly and correctly; Señora Abe Ja would have been proud! Ms. Sontag wrote "El Vuelo" on the board as she revealed the name of the composition.

With only fifteen minutes remaining in the school day, now it was Ms. Sontag's opportunity to make a special presentation.

One by one, the children were called to the front of the room to receive a certificate of participation in the science fair, as well as an individual award created by Ms. Sontag. In addition, each received two packages. One contained a yoyo styled to look like a ladybug, the other a T-shirt handmade by the teacher with personal messages about each child.

There remained just one last piece of official business: the butterfly lottery. Ms. Sontag entered the names of all of the contenders on scraps of white paper. Placing them inside a small plastic can, she shook it up and began pulling out names.

"José Luis ... Veronica ..."

"YES ... YES ... YES, YES, YES! I GOT A BUTTERFLY!" Shouting with high-pitched glee, Veronica leaped out of her chair and jumped up and down. She was too overwhelmed with joy to pay attention to the names of Wendell and Amber, the other winners.

In the small hallway near the saloncito, children were lining up. Only Ms. Sontag stood between them and the end of second grade. "Okay, I want to thank you guys for a super year," she said. "I'm so glad that each and every one of you were in this class, and I'm going to miss you a lot. And if you want to, you can write me over the summer. Or I'll give you my telephone number and you can call me anytime. You guys should be so proud of yourselves. You were such a super, super class. Really."

"Thank you, Ms. Sontag."

"Thank you."

"Thank you."

The chorus of *thank you*s spilled out the door and into the hallway. Only Dylan remained to load up his plastic container with beetles and oatmeal. Veronica's prize butterfly remained along with the others; the children would take their insects home on Wednesday.

Three unclaimed Ziplocs full of insectos de algodoncillo remained hanging from the corkboard strip. A few minutes before dismissal, Ms. Sontag and several of the children had seen them mating. A few eggs were spotted in one of the bags that very afternoon. If this information became public, she would probably have more than a few requests for adoption.

On Wednesday morning the children returned to Inter-American in the midst of a cool rain. Veronica danced around small puddles in the pavement. She carried a butterfly house made of see-through plastic in delicious anticipation of carrying home Jazmin, her new pet, along with a plant full of oruguitas. The caterpillars, she theorized, would eventually become butterflies. Which would lay eggs. Which would ultimately become more butterflies. And the cycle would continue indefinitely, supplying her with a lifetime of beautiful insects. According to Veronica, Jazmin's descendants would outlive us all.

It was the last official day of school, a day of bare walls and empty cubbys, of saying goodbye to the clutter of kids' projects, the organized disarray of childhood. Desks were pushed together to form an oversized table, with globes and papers scattered on top. Small chairs were stacked in piles amid bins of books.

An empty space had been created by the departure of the beetles, most of which were now vanquished to the far reaches of Dylan's home. Today he informed Ms. Sontag that a few had escaped and were probably hanging out in the library. When her face registered a look of shock, Dylan helpfully suggested that she start next year by asking her new students to search for insects.

Ms. Sontag sat on the floor strumming her guitar, her twelve remaining students clustered around her, singing the year away with songs about frogs and bugs. As the music continued, children and parents trickled into the room, first Marisol and her mother, María, with younger brother Wilfredo and baby sister Anita. Liset was next, then Beatríz, and finally Wendell, all with moms in tow.

A few first-graders wandered in with their parents to get a sneak preview of second grade. The janitor, who had not yet been told about the escaped beetles, smiled and swayed to the rhythm of the music. He thanked the children for keeping their room clean all year, then wished them a safe summer.

Dylan made one final, ill-fated attempt to find the runaway beetles. Ms. Sontag convinced Manny to take home the remaining packs of milkweed bugs. Luckily nobody asked about the silkworms, the gusanos de seda that had hatched out of the rock-eggs and now lay lifeless in their cardboard box. One butterfly escaped and was never seen again, but Amber was going to New York for the summer anyway. Veronica told her that if the oruguitas grew up and turned into butterflies, she could come by and pick some up when she returned.

Finally, Ms. Sontag distributed the report cards, and the class flowed through the hallway, down the stairs, and into summer.

Teachers as Artists and Intellectuals

It is hard to say who enjoyed the final days in Room 307 more, Ms. Sontag or her students. Teachers at Inter-American are not technicians who merely administer drills and lead children in memory exercises. Nor do they follow a tightly managed script. While the school has a defined philosophy and curricular guidelines, within this framework teachers are encouraged to learn and grow, to devise their own lessons, and to maximize creativity in the classroom. In other words, they are encouraged in their own intellectual development, just like the children. What's more, they are expected to enjoy themselves in the process.

Like few other species, human beings are *paedomorphic.* That is, according to animal behaviorists, we retain certain juvenile characteristics—playfulness, in particular—even after reaching adulthood. Naturally, as seventy-year-olds, we are less energetic than seven-year-olds; yet we still find ways to adapt play to fit our physical conditions and lifestyles. Play has long been recognized as a powerful vehicle for learning in children. But it should also be seen as a natural activity for adults, including teachers, not to mention an effective pedagogical tool. That's why taking play out of the classroom, an inevitable by-product of today's "data-driven reform," is counterproductive for academic growth.

Long before Professional Learning Communities became a buzzword in education, the Inter-American faculty decided to structure the school week in a way that would allow for group planning sessions, both grade-level and school-wide. Students were released early on Friday to give their teachers time for collaboration and discussion. This time was also used for professional development sessions. Teachers and administrators were encouraged to share their expertise at local, state-level, and national conferences and to contribute to the academic literature. Some went back to universities for advanced degrees, while others engaged in the arts, participating in events such as musical concerts. Collectively they held conferences at Inter-American on weekends, presenting workshops for colleagues from elsewhere. Thus their school became a center of knowledge, creativity, and inspiration not only for the Inter-American community, but also for many other educators in the Chicago area.

PART III

Outcomes

YEAR AFTER YEAR, STANDARDIZED TEST scores for Inter-American students were among the highest in Chicago, even though a sizable percentage of the children came from low-income and minority households. Naturally this was a source of pride, not to mention validation of the school's unique approach to teaching and learning—which, unlike the curriculum at most urban schools, involved little direct test preparation. It was an enviable accomplishment. Yet there were other student "outcomes" that mattered more to Inter-American parents and educators.

What were these outcomes, which were prized more highly than stellar performance on reading and math exams? Bilingualism and biculturalism, of course. These were the primary goals that the school had made explicit since its founding. But there were other payoffs, too: independent thinking abilities, appreciation of diverse groups, a sense of social justice, and positive identity construction—none of which is easily quantified, but whose ultimate value is enormous. This is what the Inter-American community had in mind when it resolved "to promote the social, affective, and cognitive development of the whole child."

❦ CHAPTER EIGHT ❦

Schooling for Life

> *The principal goal of education ... should be creating men [and women] who are capable of doing new things, not simply repeating what other generations have done —[people] who are creative, inventive, and discoverers. The second goal of education is to form minds which can be critical, can verify, and not accept everything they are offered.*
>
> —Jean Piaget

IN TODAY'S CLIMATE of test-based accountability, it's easy to forget that what matters most for kids is not how they score in the early grades, but how their schools prepare them for life. That theme featured prominently in our interviews with Inter-American alumni, including several of the students featured in the narratives above. Ms. Sontag's second-graders—now in their early twenties—have taken a variety of paths. Some are starting careers, while others are traveling, finishing college, or continuing other forms of education. Yet, like other graduates we spoke with, they all share a conviction that the Inter-American experience has had a significant impact on their choices and opportunities.

All those interviewed, without exception, remain speakers of Spanish as well as English. And all continue to use both languages, if not on a daily basis, at least for significant purposes in their lives. Quite a contrast to the experience of most Americans who studied a foreign language in school! Proficient bilingualism has enabled many Inter-American graduates to live, work, or travel in Spanish-speaking countries. Several are using Spanish on the job in the United States as translators, community advocates, businesspeople, or bilingual teachers. A few have gone on to acquire additional languages.

All of those interviewed expressed appreciation, in one way or another, for what—at least in this country—remains an unusual gift. An African-American male graduate, who started at Inter-American as an English monolingual, was typical:

> I have traveled to places and met people I would not have traveled to or met because of my Spanish. I also feel that voicing my thoughts in another language helps my mind stay sharp and really makes me value communication. Spanish is a more practical language sometimes; some things are easier said ... the Spanish really captures the intent.*

Another alumnus from an English-dominant background added:

> At Inter-American we didn't learn much grammar, but we did learn to think and dream in Spanish, thus getting to benefit from the most beautiful thing about a different language, which is a different outlook on life.

The school also helped students who were native Spanish speakers to retain the language, unlike many of their relatives. One Latino male graduate of Room 307 credited Inter-American for his ability to communicate well, not only with his parents but also with relatives in South America. Losing Spanish, he said, would have meant losing his identity and made him feel like a "whitewashed Hispanic."

Several alumni also mentioned the cross-cultural awareness that bilingualism helps to facilitate. "Inter-American was a big part of my life," recalled another of Ms. Sontag's former students. "By introducing me to Spanish, it made me feel culturally, artistically, politically, and emotionally attached to Latin America."

Equally important, the school has fostered egalitarian values and a commitment to serving others. A white female graduate now works at

---

*For extended excerpts from the interviews, see Sharon Adelman Reyes, *Student Voices from a Dual Immersion School* (forthcoming).

an immigrant rights organization that serves Spanish-speaking clients. A Puerto Rican alumna believes that fluency in Spanish will help her become an effective neighborhood organizer in Chicago. A Black Latina is studying medical anthropology as part of her plan to provide health care overseas.

Beyond bilingualism and biculturalism, Inter-American offered a curriculum that stimulated children's appetite for learning. As they look back, graduates use words like *creativity, independence, confidence, freethinking,* and *problem-solving* to describe what they remember most about their experience. These qualities have had an obvious impact on their educational and career choices.

Where Are They Now?

IT HAS BEEN FIFTEEN YEARS NOW since our story took place. Surprisingly, we were still able to track down most of the characters and to learn about the paths their lives have taken. Here, in alphabetical order, is what we can report today about Ms. Sontag's former students, the 1995–96 classmates of Room 307:

Amber worked as an AmeriCorps volunteer doing environmental projects in the Southwest before attending a British university, where she recently graduated with a degree in politics and Spanish. After living in Spain for a year during her studies, she now teaches English at a university in Chile.

Andy graduated from a liberal arts college in the Midwest with a degree in political science. Today he works as an admissions counselor there while considering graduate studies in arts administration.

Beatríz is working in health care in the Southwest while attending community college.

Camilo earned his bachelor's degree at an Illinois university, majoring in secondary education. In the summer of 2011, he was considering whether to teach high-school history or to pursue a career in nursing. While working outdoors on a hot day, he tragically and unexpectedly collapsed. Camilo will be remembered as a kind, generous, and considerate person who cared deeply for others. "He was nothing but joy," Ms. Sontag recalled, "and loved by all his classmates."

César is employed full-time at an insurance firm while studying accounting at a Chicago-area university.

Damion attended the U.S. Military Academy at West Point, but left after deciding that army life was not for him. He is now attending a community college in the Northeast, while working in a restaurant and planning a career in sports management and physical therapy.

Dylan took time off between high school and college, traveling and volunteering to help victims of Hurricane Katrina in New Orleans (where he encountered Amber doing similar work). Today he lives in the Northeast, completing undergraduate degrees from two different universities, in liberal arts and mechanical engineering.

Enrique graduated from a liberal arts college in Chicago, with a concentration in marketing and communications and a minor in art direction. He now works in the airline industry while thinking about graduate school in American history or economics.

Joaquin recently graduated from a police academy and is working for a university police force in Illinois.

José Luis is studying architecture at a university in the Southwest while also pursuing his interest in photography.

Leticia won a four-year scholarship to a Midwestern university and spent her junior year abroad studying in Spain. Since graduating, she has worked in advertising, using her Spanish on a daily basis. She hopes to go back to school soon to get her M.B.A.

Manny serves as the leadership program facilitator at an independent school in Illinois that serves low-income children in grades 2–8 who face serious hardships due to disrupted families and communities. In addition, since earning an associate's degree in food and beverage management, he has worked as a self-employed chef. Meanwhile, he is studying business at a Chicago-area university.

Marisol graduated from a liberal arts college on the East Coast with a double major in Spanish and Italian.

Naomi studied Mandarin for four years in high school, traveling to Beijing and living with a Chinese family. While attending a Chicago-area university, she returned to China and spent her sophomore year studying Chinese language, culture, philosophy, history, and music. On returning to the United States, she has continued her international studies program with an emphasis on Asia.

Veronica is completing her undergraduate degree in psychology at a university in the Northwest, along with a certification in early-childhood education, while working full-time in a bilingual (Spanish-English) preschool.

Finally, what about *Jill Sontag,* whose lasting influence on her former students is widely acknowledged? We are happy to report that she is still working in public education. A few years after our story ended, she won the prestigious Golden Apple Award for Outstanding Teaching. Today she serves as bilingual lead teacher and dual language coordinator at the Whittier Elementary School in Chicago, where Inter-American's former reading specialist, Zoila García, is principal. Ms. Sontag remains part of an exceptional professional community.

Source Notes

❧ ❧ ❧

Page

1   *"a sense of hope ..."*   Mike Rose, *Possible Lives: The Promise of Public Education in America* (New York: Penguin Books, 2006), p. xvii.

2   *ethnographic study*   Sharon Adelman Reyes, "'¡Mami, yo toqué una mariposa!' An Alternative to Linguistic and Cultural Loss" (PH.D. diss., University of Illinois, Chicago, 1998).

7   *"Knowing a second language ..."*   Kendall King and Alison Mackey, *The Bilingual Edge: Why, When, and How to Teach Your Child a Second Language* (New York: Collins, 2007), p. 252.

7   *even cognitive*   Fergus I. M. Craik, Ellen Bialystok, and Morris Freedman, "Delaying the Onset of Alzheimer Disease: Bilingualism as a Form of Cognitive Reserve," *Neurology* 75 (2010): 1726–29.

8   *much better at actual communication*   Jim Cummins, "Research Findings from French Immersion Programs across Canada," in Colin Baker and Nancy Hornberger, eds., *An Introductory Reader to the Writings of Jim Cummins* (Clevedon, U.K.: Multilingual Matters, 2001), pp. 96–105.

9   *"317,000 Anglophone students*   Statistics Canada, "Public School Indicators for Canada, the Provinces and Territories, 2000/2001 to 2008/2009"; online: http://www.statcan.gc.ca/pub/81-004-x/2011001/article/11433-eng.htm.

10   *need to learn only once*   Stephen Krashen, *Under Attack:*
       The Case Against Bilingual Education (Culver City, Calif.:
       Language Education Associates, 1996), pp. 25–27.

11   *primarily in their native language*   Cheryl Urow and Jill
       Sontag, "Creating Community—Un Mundo Entero: The
       Inter-American Experience," in Donna Christian and Fred
       Genesee, eds., *Bilingual Education* (Alexandria, Va.:
       Teachers of English to Speakers of Other Languages, 2001),
       pp. 12–25.

11   *dual immersion model during the 1995–96 school year*
       Kim Potowski, *Language and Identity in a Dual Language*
       School (Clevedon, U.K.: Multilingual Matters, 2007).

11   *well above city and state norms*   Donna Christian,
       Christopher J. Montone, Kathryn J. Lindholm, and Isolda
       Carranza, *Profiles in Two-Way Immersion Education*
       (Washington, D.C.: Center for Applied Linguistics and Delta
       Systems, 1997).

11   *have often proved superior*   Katherine J. Lindholm-Leary,
       Dual Language Education (Clevedon, U.K.: Multilingual
       Matters, 2001).

12   *"one fundamental way ... "*   Stephen Krashen quoted in
       James Crawford, *Educating English Learners: Language*
       Diversity in the Classroom, 5th ed. (Los Angeles: Bilingual
       Educational Services, 2004), p. 189.

13   *"something that a learner does ... "*   Beverly Falk, *Teaching*
       the Way Children Learn (New York: Teachers College Press,
       2009), p. 26.

14   *zone of proximal development*   L. S. Vygotsky, *Mind in*
       Society: The Development of Higher Psychological Processes
       (Cambridge, Mass.: Harvard University Press, 1978).

15   *"Knowing is a process ... "*   Jerome S. Bruner, *Toward a*
       Theory of Instruction (Cambridge, Mass.: Harvard
       University Press, 1966), p. 72.

15   *i + 1*   Stephen D. Krashen, *The Input Hypothesis: Issues and Implications* (London: Longman, 1985).

16   *"Constructivism is derived ..."*   Alfie Kohn, *The Schools Our Children Deserve: Moving Beyond Traditional Classrooms and "Tougher Standards"* (Boston: Houghton Mifflin, 1999), pp. 132–33.

17   *"Reading the world ..."*   Paulo Freire and Donaldo Macedo, *Literacy: Reading the Word and the World* (South Hadley, Mass.: Bergin & Garvey Publishers, 1987), p. 23.

19   *"an idea with revolutionary implications ..."*   Deborah Meier, *The Power of Their Ideas: Lessons for America from a Small School in Harlem* (Boston: Beacon Press, 1995), p. 4.

19   *"[Y]ou who are wise ..."*   *The Writings of Benjamin Franklin* (New York: MacMillan, 1907), vol. 10, pp. 98–99.

20   *practices, both subtle and obvious*   Guadalupe Valdes, "Dual-Language Immersion Programs: A Cautionary Note Concerning the Education of Language-Minority Students," *Harvard Educational Review* 67 (Fall 1997): 391–429.

23   *"a theory about learning ..."*   Catherine Twomey Fosnot, *Constructivism: Theory, Perspectives, and Practice*, 2nd ed. (New York: Teachers College Press, 2005), p. 33.

23   *clear implications in the classroom*   Sharon Adelman Reyes and Trina Lynn Vallone, *Constructivist Strategies for Teaching English Language Learners* (Thousand Oaks, Calif.: Corwin Press, 2008).

23   *"The pupil's mind is a growing organism ..."*   Alfred North Whitehead, *The Aims of Education and Other Essays* (New York: Simon and Schuster, 1967), p. 30.

24   *"habits of mind ..."*   Meier, *The Power of Their Ideas*, p. 50.

26   *"most worthwhile to know and experience ..."*   William H. Schubert, "Historical Perspective on Centralizing

Curriculum," in M. Frances Klein, ed., *The Politics of Curriculum Decision-Making: Issues in Centralizing the Curriculum* (Albany, N.Y.: SUNY Press, 1991), p. 114.

40   ***Free voluntary reading***   Stephen Krashen, *Free Voluntary Reading* (Santa Barbara, Calif.: Libraries Unlimited, 2011).

43   ***Other grades studied the Incas***   Cindy Zucker, "The Role of ESL in a Dual Language Program," *Bilingual Research Journal* 19 (Summer/Fall 1995): 513–23.

90   ***"Once you can read ..."***   Krashen, *Under Attack*, p. 4.

104   ***human beings are paedomorphic***   Patricia B. McConnell, *The Other End of the Leash* (New York: Ballantine Books), p. 88.

109   ***"The principal goal of education ..."***   Jean Piaget quoted in Evans Clinchy, "Different Drummers and Teacher Training," *Education Week*, Feb. 4, 1998.

Acknowledgments

During the year of research at Inter-American, if the phone sometimes rang too early in the morning, I could be certain it was Jill Sontag.

"Hurry, Sharon," she might say, and then inform me about some newsworthy second-grade event. "Another insect jail-break has occurred," for example. Or, "Alicia discovered caterpillars in the butterfly cage!"

Then, like a schoolchild myself, I would rush over to Inter-American, eating breakfast in the car and readying my audio cassette, pen, and notepaper as I scrambled up the stairs to Room 307.

Sometimes the roles were reversed. "You will never believe what Naomi was doing while you were discussing insect care," I might say. "She was working on a secret art project inside her desk." Or, "Dylan and Manny were painting each other's shirts again, instead of the mural." Naturally, she would never let on to the children that I had reported such things. It was just an opportunity for a good laugh at the end of a hectic day for both of us.

The children of Room 307 were also gracious hosts. They shared their inventions and discoveries with me, and occasionally begged for answers they were supposed to figure out for themselves. Usually, I refused to give in.

Despite my explanations, most of them never quite understood why I was in their classroom, but they obviously enjoyed my presence. Some saw me as just another Inter-American mom, one who liked to hang out in classrooms and tape interviews. Others theorized that I worked at the school. But whatever the children believed, we had plenty of fun together. For the first time in my life, I was sorry to see the coming of summer vacation.

Not only did I enjoy my time in Room 307. My entire year at Inter-American was rewarding in other ways. The potluck dinners, hallway conversations with parents and teachers, curriculum nights, student assemblies, a seemingly endless array of cultural events, and families' involvement in all aspects of the school added up to a profound sense of connectedness.

While I knew the Inter-American community would still be there the following September, my daughter and her classmates would be reconfigured into the third grade. This year's unique blend of children, led on paths of discovery by an exceptional teacher, could never occur again. So when that experience was over, I felt both joy and sadness and, of course, gratitude for the opportunity to document it.

Above all else, we thank Jill Sontag and her students for sharing one joyful and unforgettable year in their lives.

For generously assisting us in various ways to share that experience with our readers, we thank Zoila García, Lois La Galle, Gina La Ruffa, Glenna Adelman Reyes, Anastasia Skolnik, Cheryl Urow, and Wendy Villegas.

Finally, for reviewing the manuscript and offering prompt and insightful commentary, we express our appreciation to Graciela A. Christensen, Mary Carol Combs, Stephen Krashen, Jill Sontag, and Trina Lynn Vallone.

About *DiversityLearningK12*

Specializing in bilingual, ESL, and multicultural education, DiversityLearningK12 is a consulting group that provides professional development, keynote presentations, program design, educational publishing, and related services. For more information, please visit us at www.diversitylearningk12.com or email us at info@diversitylearningk12.com.

CPSIA information can be obtained
at www.ICGtesting.com
Printed in the USA
LVOW12s0108130916

504349LV00001B/13/P